CAITHNESS

A PEEK INTO THE PAST

It was not often in Caithness that trees were blown over to block a road – not enough trees perhaps – but this one at Dunbeath interrupted traffic on the A9 in the great gale in February 1953.

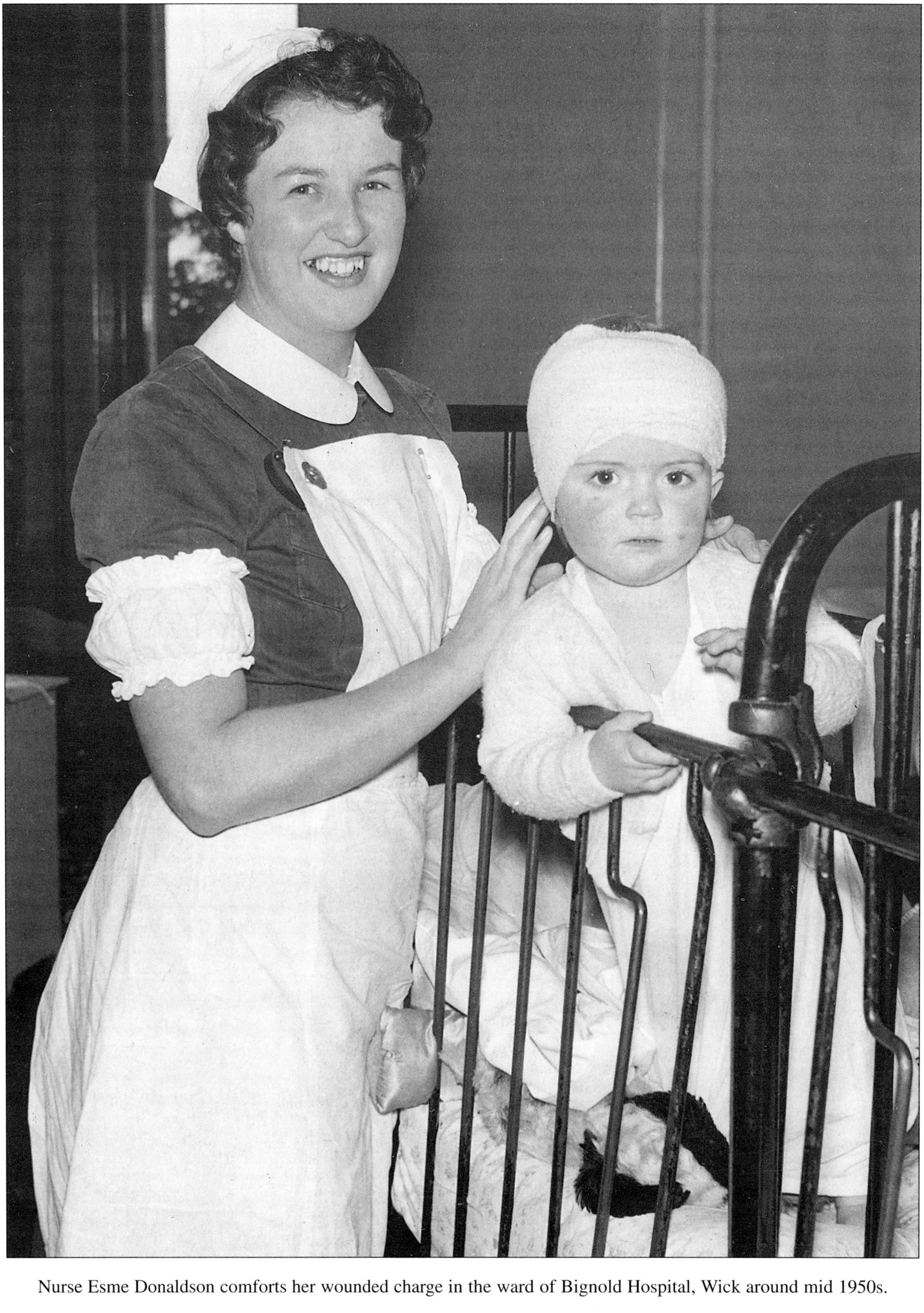

Nurse Esme Donaldson comforts her wounded charge in the ward of Bignold Hospital, Wick around mid 1950s.

CAITHNESS

A PEEK INTO THE PAST

A NOSTALGIC LOOK AT YESTERDAY'S CAITHNESS

Compiled by
Clive Richards

Published by
North of Scotland
NEWSPAPERS
Wick, Caithness, Scotland

Acknowledgements

This book preparation has involved many individuals. Their assistance is gratefully acknowledged. Our heartflet thanks and appreciation are expressed to our friend James Miller whose contribution and hours of hard work made this book possible.

We express our deep gratitude to those fine people who have responded to our appeal for photographs of family, friends and memorable places, and who have demonstrated in words and deeds the true meaning of sharing.

Grateful acknowledgement is made for the copyright photographs of Maurice Harrington, Northern Studios, J. McDonald, Mario Luciani and J. Baikie, Stromness, the U.K.A.E.A. and, above all a special tribute to the late John Adams whose remarkable images adorn the pages of this publication.

A Catalogue Record for this book is available from The British Library.

ISBN 1 871704 32 4

Cover by Naver Limited, Thurso, Caithness.

Photocomposed by North of Scotland Newspapers, 42 Union Street, Wick, Caithness, Scotland.
Printed by Highland Printers, Henderson Road, Inverness, Scotland.

A family scrapbook for the county: Caithness

To any stranger coming north along the A9 road, the sweep of cliff-bound coast extending into the distance from Dunbeath, a rugged boundary between rolling plain to the west and the grey miles of the Moray Firth, is a promise of difference. Caithness is frontier country, a land of contrasts, a place where Celt and Norseman meet, where Lowland rubs against Highland.

Nostalgia and childhood are often inseparable. Our memories of the past are memories of younger versions of ourselves.

Cousins Elizabeth Munro from Harpsdale Mains and Christine Munro from Houstry Mains enjoy an al fresco tea in Halkirk in 1968. *(Submitted by Linda Munro, Halkirk).*

View of the coast north from Dunbeath.

Enthusiasm and determination are plainly visible on the faces of these entrants in the girl's race at Dunbeath Highland Games in July, 1952.

CONTENTS

Introduction
Operation Snowdrop 10
Gala Days 20
Sport...38
Sport of a kind............................48
A time of transition 52
Stroma – end of an island 53
Dounreay – a new industry 60
Other industries 68
General Election – 1955 70
Altnabreac scheme.......................71
Transport 75
Local progress 82
Dounreay visitors.........................86
The Royal connection 89
The land......................................92
The sea......................................102
Schooldays through the ages 110
The daily round 119
On stage 150
Let's dance................................155
From the family album 170

Coopers and, in the background, herring gutters and packers gave this demonstration of their various skills at a pageant at Wick riverside in August, 1953.

THE GOOD OLD DAYS

The visual journey presented in this book is a trip through time. Most of the images are from the portfolio of John Cyril Percy Adams, who had his studio in Wick from 1946 to 1966. During his time in Caithness, he formed a close friendship with David Oag, the editor of the *John O'Groat Journal*, in whose pages many of John Adam's news photography was published.

Most of the images in this book first appeared in the weekly issues of the paper during the 1950s and '60s.

The Adams collection has been supplemented here by photographs by Thurso photographer, Maurice Harrington, and many pictures contributed by members of the public. Most depict scenes from the 1950s and '60s, although a few are from much further back in time.

Enjoy the trip.

THE BLEAK MIDWINTER OF 1955

Operation Snowdrop

On 12 January 1955, the north of Scotland was hit by a blizzard of unusual ferocity. In a short space of time, two trains became stuck at Bower, a BEA aircraft with twenty passengers was stranded on the runway at Wick, vehicles were abandoned along many roads, several schools closed, and villages and farms were isolated. More snow and drifting in the 60 mph winds hampered attempts to keep roads open and the RAF and the Royal Navy were called in to help the local authorities maintain services and bring in food, fuel and fodder. The aircraft carrier HMS *Glory* took up station in Loch Eriboll to act as a base, along with Wick, to coordinate the rescue and relief operations.

The first phase of bad weather lasted for 16 days and then, on 17 February, a second blizzard began – worse than the first, thought many, as the wind gusted to over 70mph and 10-foot drifts piled across the roads. The final thaw did not set in until the first days of March. On the 3rd the trains were back in operation but the RAF was still dropping food and fodder to farms.

The two blizzards have melted into one in most people's memories – all encapsulated in the words 'Operation Snowdrop'.

The view of a main road from the cab of the Council snowplough.

The same snowplough trying to find the way through.

Above, conditions were almost as bad in Hill Avenue, Wick.
(Submitted by Ella, Wick).

Right, Bridge Street, Wick, 1955.
(Submitted by Bert Sutherland, Wick).

West Banks Avenue, Wick, early December 1956.

A casualty of the severe winter of 1955 is rescued by the crew of a Royal Naval helicopter.

Royal Naval helicopters flew many sorties to deliver food and fodder to outlying districts and isolated farms . . . *(Submitted by Ella, Wick).*

A storm of wind and snow blew this ambulance into the ditch a mile or south of Wick on 23rd December, 1954. Neither the driver nor the nurse aboard were hurt.

Above: After the storm, Bridge Street, Wick, 1955.
Right: Abandoned car.

In January, 1959, passengers had to be rescued when a bus was stranded in Watten. Clearly they were not greatly distressed by their ordeal.

A rotary snowplough tackles the drifts on the A9 near Thrumster in January, 1959.

Stuck?

GPO engineers arrive at Berriedale to repair the damaged overhead cables.
(Submitted by Bert Sutherland, Wick), (extreme right).

Passengers on this bus near Thrumster in February, 1960, try to get the vehicle moving.

More snow clearing from the A9, in February, 1960.

The new Technical College and the view across a snow-struck Thurso towards the cliffs of Dunnet Head.

Alex Coghill, milkman with Ronaldson's of Westerseat, takes a well-earned break with his horse on a demanding daily round through the snow covered streets of Wick during the winter of 1955.
(Submitted by Mrs W. Davidson of Haster, daughter of Alex Coghill).

Above: The frozen Thurso river at Halkirk.

Left: Francis Street, Wick, February, 1955.
(Submitted by Bert Sutherland, Wick).

Are you ready for this? Two young men enjoy the lighter side of the severe conditions of 1955.
(Submitted by Bert Sutherland, Wick).

Heavy rain in September, 1956, caused this flood in Union Street, Wick.

The boating pavilion caught in a flash flood in August, 1957. Two inches of rain fell in 33 hours.

Gala days

Her train, suitably a net, adorned with images of the silver darlings, Harbour Queen, Reta Shearer arrives in Wick harbour on Saturday, 17th July, 1937 on the *Drift Fisher* (Skipper James More). The ladies-in-waiting are Mary More and Catherine Miller. The three girls were chosen by their fellow senior pupils at Wick High School. Although the herring industry was in a depression in the summer of 1937, the staging of the first Herring Queen event was hailed a great success and attracted large crowds. Organised by a sub-committee of the Riverside and Town Improvements Committee, some of the profits from the celebration were donated to the Royal National Lifeboat Institution.

Below: Lady Sinclair, wife of Sir Archibald Sinclair, crowns Catherine Mackay, Lybster's first Harbour Queen, in July, 1949.

Joyce Maleham steps ashore as Wick's Herring Queen in 1951. Her escort is led by Provost Bessie Leith.

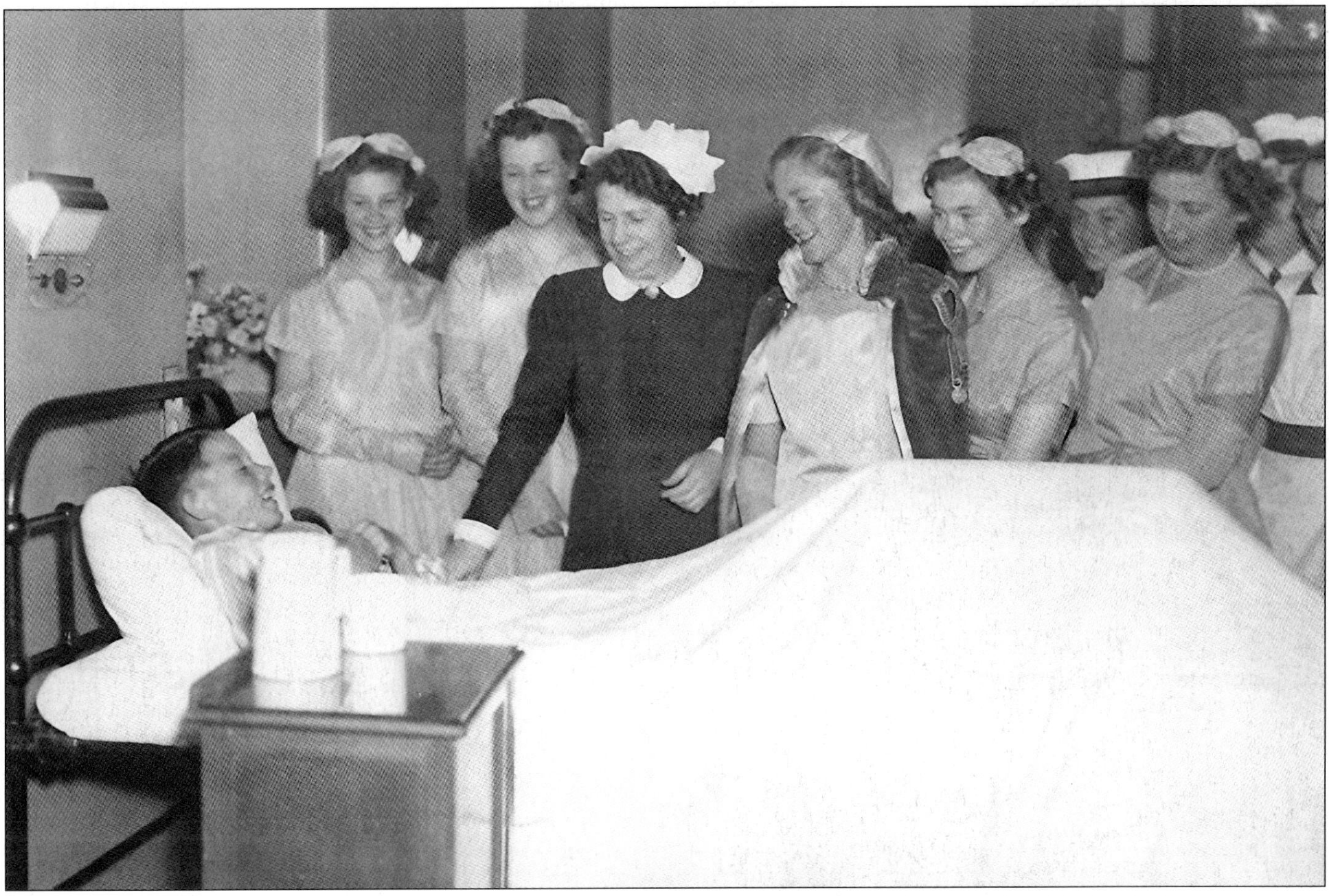

Herring Queen, Joyce Maleham, brings a laugh to a young male patient in Bignold Hospital.

Floats and fancy dress have always been features of the gala parades. A severe gale wrought £275,000 worth of damage across Caithness in the winter of 1952, and inspired this gentleman to join the Herring Queen parade in the following summer.

Marie Simpson was Herring Queen in 1952.

Halkirk chose her first British Legion Queen in 1952 with the honour falling to Rosalind Walsh.

Christine Mackay, Thurso Gala Queen in 1953, is driven though the streets.

Some of the entrants in the children's fancy dress parade at the 1953 Herring Queen festival. The boy on the extreme right below is 'Sherpa Tensing', fresh from the conquest of Mount Everest that summer. Gas masks were still plentiful from the war years.

Anne Gunn is crowned as Thurso's Gala Queen in 1955.

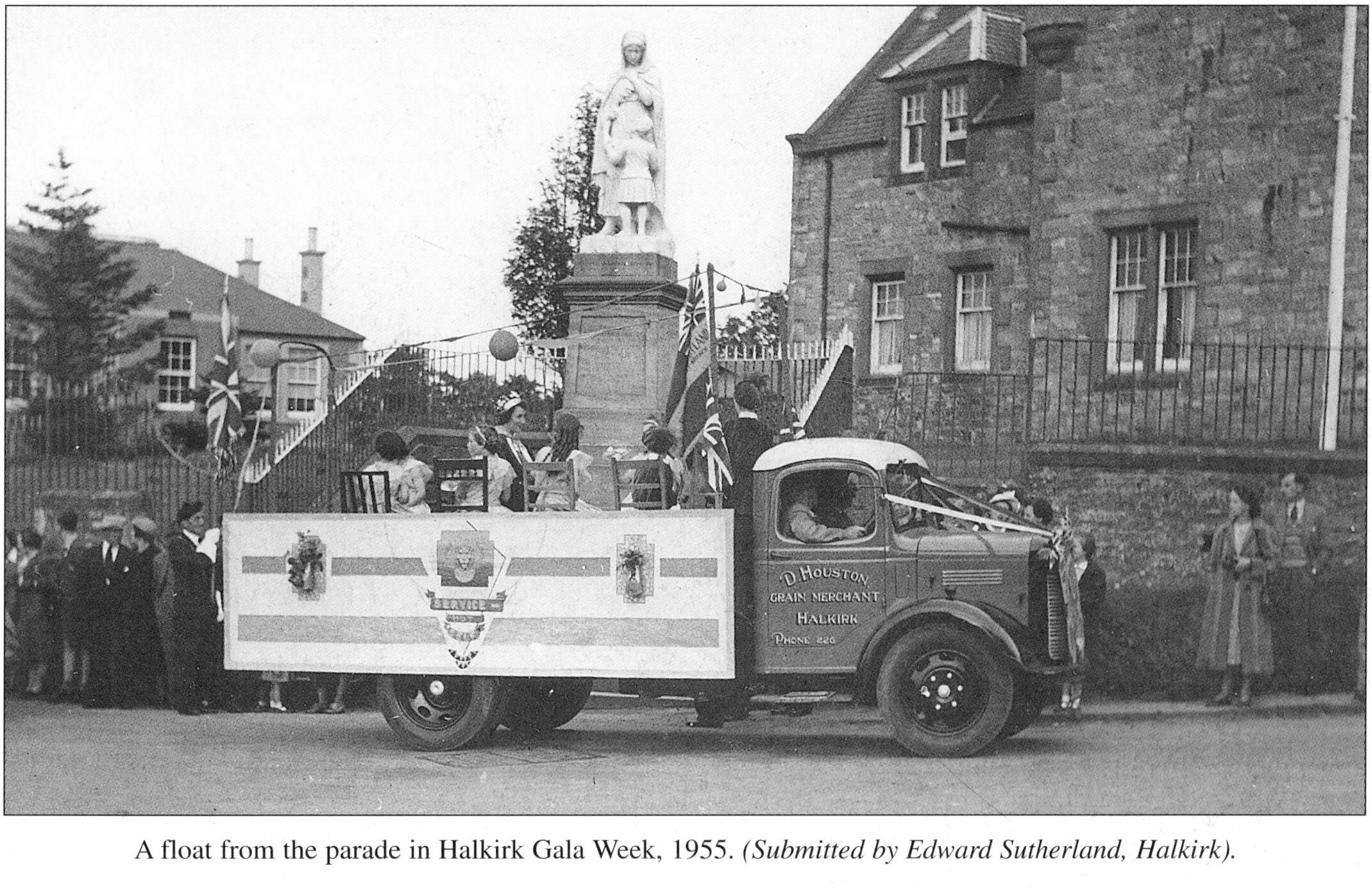

A float from the parade in Halkirk Gala Week, 1955. *(Submitted by Edward Sutherland, Halkirk).*

A tractor and trailer float from the Halkirk Gala. *(Submitted by Edward Sutherland).*

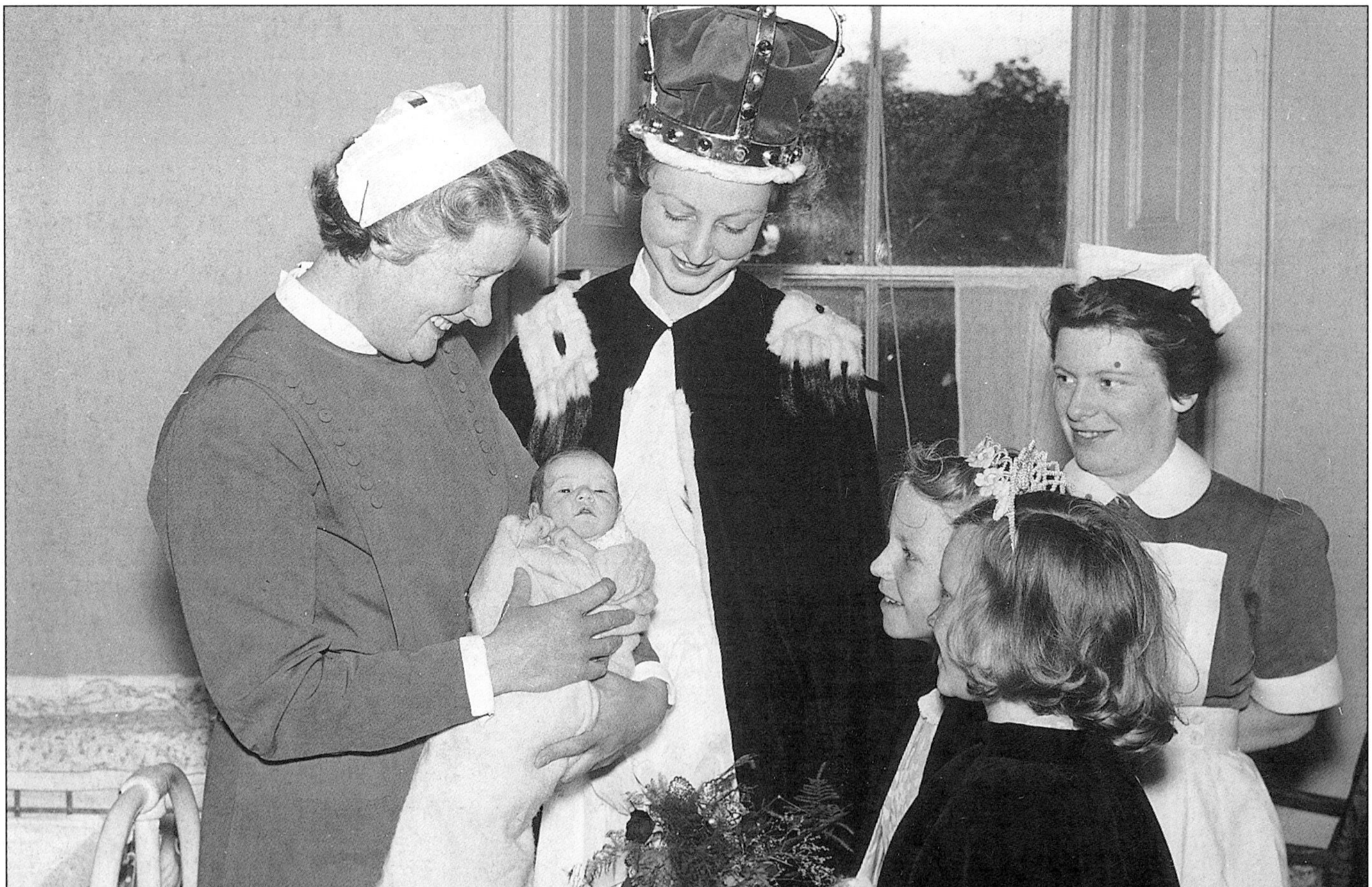

Queen Mary's two girl-pages are obviously fascinated by a baby during their visit to Dunbar Hospital.

Provost John Sinclair escorts Thurso Gala Queen, Mary Manson, and her retinue in Sir John's Square during the crowning ceremony in 1958.

Popeye is among the entrants in the Thurso fancy dress parade in 1960.

This cheery group is believed to be the contestants in an Opportunity Knocks session in Thurso Gala Week in 1960. *(Submitted by Mandy Mowat, Thurso).*

Thurso's Gala Queen in 1961 was Hilary Allan, here shown at the crowning ceremony with Provost D.K. Sutherland.

Even in 1961, the NHS was the focus of controversy, as shown in this Thurso float.

Winner of the premier award for best vehicle in the carnival procession in Wick in 1962, was this living recreation of the Commando Memorial at Spean Bridge.

This was Wick's first Gala Queen, Catherine Sinclair, pictured in 1961, after a few years of an event on a smaller scale. The Gala Queen took the place of the Herring Queen but, as a link with the past, Catherine was crowned by Reta Shearer, the first Herring Queen and now Mrs David Mackay.

In August 1962, Thurso chose a Liberal Fair Queen – June Robson

Thurso, 1963 and the horse with the queen's coach seems to be giving cause for concern.

Carnival winner at the Wick Gala on Saturday, 3rd August, 1963.

Wick 1963 – The fancy dress parade in Smith Terrace.

Halkirk Gala Queen, 1958, Ishbel Harper, with attendants, Jean Ross and Ann Green with Alex Miller on extreme right.
(Submitted by George Forbes, Halkirk). Photographer: J. McDonald.

Top left: Ann McGregor, Thurso Gala Queen, 1964.

Top right: Wick Gala Queen, 1965 – Lilian Sutherland, with attendants, Margaret Budge and Diana Watt.

Wick Provost, W.G. Mowat, escorts Gala Queen, Margaret Rendall in 1967.

1951 – Elma Gunn, first Halkirk Gala Queen, is led to the crowning ceremony by Legion chairman, George Andrew. Flag bearer, Donnie Macdonald. The tall princess is Margaret Gunn, Gerston, the other princess was Jane Gow.
(Submitted by George Forbes, Halkirk).

1951 – Elma Gunn crowned as Halkirk's first British Legion Queen (Gala Queen).
(Submitted by George Forbes, Halkirk).

Mid 1950s (probably 1956) – Halkirk Gala Queen procession down Crescent Street, towards Ross Institute.
1954 Austin A40 Pick-up (SK 4575), Dod Houston, Grain Merchant, Halkirk.
April 1954 Registration Austin A40 Pick-up (SK 4432), James Gunn, Gerston, Halkirk.
October 1955 Registration Ford Tractor (SK 4971), William Munro, Houstry. *(Submitted by George Forbes, Halkirk).*

A day out at the County Show held at the Riverside, Wick about 1953.
(Submitted by J. & V. Sutherland, Lyth).

The boys from Wick Fire Brigade enjoy a busman's holiday at a Wick Gala parade.
(Submitted by Mervyn Hill, Wick.).

The Herring Queen parade proceeds up Union Street, Wick, circa 1900. *(Submitted by Mrs W. Hastie).*

1952 – Halkirk Gala Queen, Rosalind Walsh, crowned indoors at the Ross Institute due to rain. *(Submitted by George Forbes, Halkirk).*

Halkirk Gala Week, 1955 – Sir Archibald Sinclair, guest speaker. Gala Queen: Margaret Bain, Princesses Ishbel Harper, Kathleen Farmer and Maureen Coghill. *(Submitted by George Forbes, Halkirk).*

Halkirk Gala Week 1955 – Procession of floats led by Gala Queen and attendants in lorry owned by Dod Houston, Grain Merchant. *(Submitted by George Forbes, Halkirk).*

Sport

Caithness folk have always enjoyed a wide range of sport, as these pictures testify.

Halkirk Club were very successful in 1935, winning the Rural League championship and the Paterson Cup. Back row (left to right): George Henderson, George Anderson, William Mackenzie, David Bain, Angus Munro, A. MacPherson, J.S.Sutherland (Trainer).
Front row (left to right): William (Burke) Sutherland, Hamish Sinclair, Ken McKenzie, Dugald McLarty, Murdo (Matt) Campbell, John Paul.

In the spring of 1930 competitive football between village teams was inaugurated in Caithness, and three trophies were put up as prizes. Teams were entered from Castletown, Keiss, Halkirk, Mey, Watten and Wick Boy Scouts were also allowed to take part. In 1933 John O'Groats Pentland entered the lists, and in 1935 Staxigoe came forward for the first time. The matches were played in the late spring in the evenings during the close season for senior football and were followed with keen interest. The competitions did much to foster football in the rural parts of the county.

The Scouts football team in Wick, 1947.
(Submitted by Bert Sutherland).

Thurso Acks FC celebrate their Diamond Jubilee with a dinner in November, 1958.

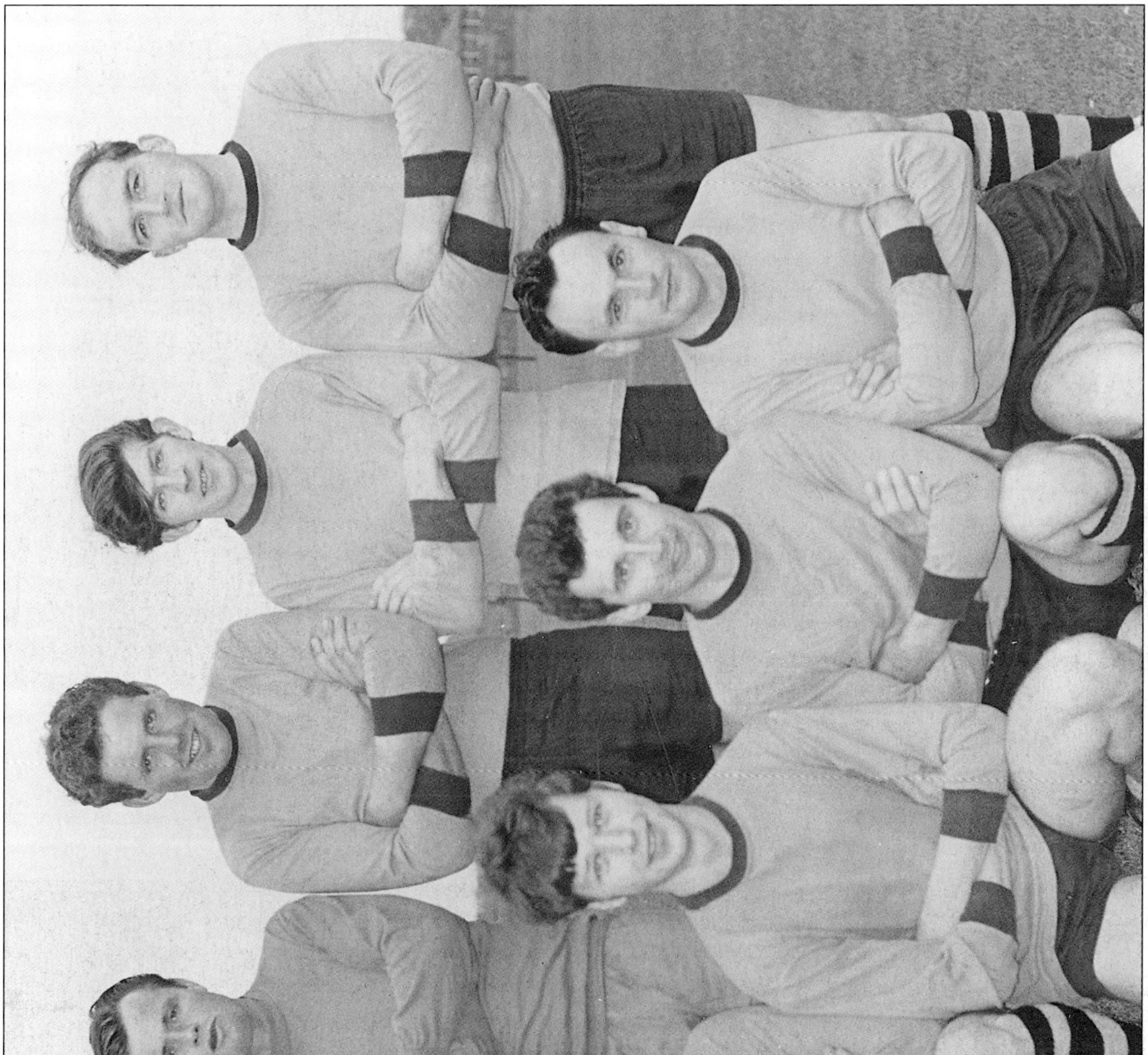

Bower football team, 1969. One of the eight teams that regularly played in the Rural League. Back row (left to right): J. Farquhar, M. Miller, D. Macleod, A. Gunn, A. Thain, A. Sutherland. Front row (left to right): H. Steven, J. Dunbar, H. Macleod, J. Swanson, W. Gunn.
(Submitted by Allan Sutherland, Bower). Photographer: M. Luciani, Thurso.

Halkirk Rifle Club, 1964. *(Submitted by James Gunn, Gerston, Halkirk).*

Rifle shooting was a popular club activity over many years. Here A.B. Bremner, captain of the Pentland Rifle Club, presents a medal to secretary, W. Shearer, on the occasion of the club's golden jubilee in February, 1960.

Christine Gunn, Gerston, urges her horse, Philip, over a fence at the Caithness County Show, held at Thurso in 1955. Philip was bought by Christine as a two-year-old from Westerseat and trained by herself to become the best jumper in the north at the time. He was named after HRH Prince Philip, Duke of Edinburgh.
(Submitted by Edward Sutheland, Halkirk).

Thurso Rifle Club, 1938. *(Submitted by Catherine Begg, Thurso).*

W. Mackay from Lybster wins the 100-yard sprint at Wick Highland Games on 19th August, 1961.

In 1961, this team of stalwarts revived the game of hockey in Wick.

Long coats and bonnets are the order of the day at the Rosebank Bowling Club when their new flag was hoisted on what was clearly a chilly day in May, 1957.

Better weather a year later (May 1958) when the members of the Rosebank club were captured for posterity.

Loch Sarclet was the regular venue for the members of the model yacht club, photographed on 26 May, 1962.
(Submitted by Maurice Harrington).

Were winters colder then? Curling enthusiasts of John O'Groats Club at Bilbster in January, 1963.

Model yachting at Sarclet with David Flett, Ronald McKain, Oag brothers and Hughie Malcolm.
(Submitted by Maurice Harrington).

Caithness Flying club lost its Auster aircraft when David Smart, the instructor, failed to clear a dyke during a tricky take-off at Niandt, Forse. Alone aboard, Mr Smart suffered only a broken tooth in this incident on 29th January, 1964.

Sport of a kind

Land's End to John O'Groats.

During the 1950s and early 1960s a craze developed to contest the record for the journey - usually on foot - between Land's End and John O'Groats. One of the earliest record breakers was, however, a cyclist, Eileen Sheridan from Coventry, who pedalled the distance of 871 miles in 2 days, 11 hours and 7 minutes. She arrived at Groats at 9 p.m. on Sunday, 11th July, 1954. After two hours of sleep she mounted her bike again to go for the 1,000-mile record and finished the successful attempt at 11 a.m. on Monday - her total time was 3 days and one hour.

Peter Hoy from Manchester arrived at Land's End on 31st January, 1960, 19 days and 14 hours after leaving Groats.

Another hopeful contestant, Charles Benson from Essex, left Groats on 9th February, 1960. John Adams caught him turning from High Street into Bridge Street.

Two Sussex youths try to beat the Land's End to John O'Groats record in May, 1961, they failed by $4\frac{1}{2}$ hours.

In March, 1960, in a snowstorm, over 700 contestants set out from John O'Groats to attempt the walk to Lands End in a competition organised by Billy Butlin, the holiday camp magnet, with prizes of £5,000. Only 138 completed the course.

Relay teams also competed. Here Alan Ross, captain of a team from Reading Athletic Club, arrives at the John O'Groats House Hotel, in April, 1960. The team set a new record of 87 hours 5 minutes.

Councillor John S. Banks about to send off the first three runners in the Boys Brigade relay from Groats to the Lord Mayor of London to publicise their HQ Appeal Fund in May, 1961.

The long walk was open to anyone and attracted many characters to give it a go. Gustave de Jonckheere, who was a resident of Stonehaven, was 73-years-old when he set off on 5th April, 1962. He reached Land's End on the evening of Sunday, 29th April.

On 3rd July, 1962, runners from Cambridge University Hares and Hounds Club started their attempt on the relay record on a south-bound run. Their winning time was 82 hours 42 minutes. In this picture, Tim Johnston sets off.

1950s - 60s – a time of transition

Caithness saw a number of important changes in its social and economic life during the 1950s and '60s. The old ways, based on farming and fishing, continued but now new industries and activities sprang up.

One early change was the electrification of the rural areas as the generating and distribution schemes of the North of Scotland Hydro-Electric Board gradually spread across the north. Many villages staged switch-on ceremonies to mark the arrival of "the electric". This scene is from the ceremony in January, 1954, at Melvich, where the postmistress, Miss M. Mackintosh, was presented with an electric kettle by Mr T. Lawrie, the general manager of the Board.

Stroma – end of an island

In the middle of the Pentland Firth, Stroma was often cut off by heavy seas. *(Submitted by Stuart Sinclair, Thurso).*

Stroma, seen here from the top of the Warth Hill, lost almost all its people in the 1950s as economic opportunities encouraged them to move to the mainland. John Adam's picture is undated but the landscape is typical of the early 1950s, with its untarred side roads and fields being cultivated by traditional methods.

The main road across Stroma on a wet day. The long white building on the skyline is the Co-op store.
This image is redolent of rural life in the 1950s.
(Submitted by J. Sinclair, Wick). Photographer: W. S. Baikie, Stromness.

Stroma acquired a much improved harbour in the 1950s. Here are some of the men who were engaged on the project. *(Submitted by Stuart Sinclair).*

The new harbour not far from completion.
(Submitted by J. Sinclair).

Two Stroma fishermen, Malkie Simpson at the tiller and Dan Sinclair. Malkie left the island for Thurso in June, 1955, and in October that same year, Dan and his family moved to Keiss. The boat was the *Evelyn.*
(Submitted by Stuart Sinclair).

The Haven Stroma – About the time the new harbour was being built in the 1950s.
(Submitted by J. Sinclair).

The construction of the Stroma foghorn with John Jolly Sinclair pictured right, circa 1930.
(Submitted by Stuart Sinclair).

Grimsby trawler, *Mars*, aground at Langatoun, Stroma, in 1930. She ran aground in thick fog and one man, the cook, was lost. The skipper was an Icelander by the name of Goodmund. *(Submitted by Stuart Sinclair).*

Stroma islanders did not burn peat, so the coal boat, *Ashdene*, came once a year to unload tons of coal on the quayside. All able-bodied men bagged the coal and delivered the required amount to each household. The photograph was taken before the new harbour was built. *(Submitted by J. Sinclair).*

The annual arrival of the coalboat in Stroma harbour under construction. *(Submitted by Stuart Sinclair).*

Johnnie Sinclair, manager, and Jessie Smith outside the SCWS shop on Stroma. This was the start of Jessie's long career with the Co-op.
(Submitted by J. Sinclair).

Three Stroma men photographed in the 1930s. Pictured centre, Sybil McCaughey's father, George Manson.
(Submitted by D. Manson).

Sybil McCaughey (née Manson), on the knee of her uncle, Malky Manson, on Stroma in August, 1924.
(Submitted by D. Manson).

Dounreay – a new industry

The announcement on 1st March, 1954, that the experimental fast-breeder reactor establishment of the United Kingdom Atomic Energy Authority was to be located at the former second-world-war airfield at Dounreay, caused great excitement in Caithness. At the time there was almost no apprehension of the implications of becoming economically wedded to the industry, and everyone looked forward to a new age of prosperity.

Construction at Dounreay began in March, 1955, and the first phase was largely complete by the end of 1958. A prototype fast reactor was built between 1967 and 1974.

Thurso in the 1920s was a small, quiet town with a population of some 2,000. By 1951, the population had risen to a little over 3,000. Dounreay was to precipitate a period of rapid growth and in the 1961 census the number of inhabitants had risen to 8,276.

(Submitted by Mrs Finella MacKinnon).

This photograph was taken from what is now a louvred 'window' in the church tower of St. Peter's and St. Andrew's, church facing Sir John's Square. It seems the photograph was taken between 1906 and 1916 - on a cold winter's day. Note the drinking fountain at the far end of the square which is now sited at the top end on Princes Street to make way for the War Memorial. Many of the buildings remain relatively unchanged, but Fraser's Tearooms and Bakery was demolished prior to 1916 to allow the Post Office to be built.
Compare with the picture below taken in September, 2004.

The opening ceremony of the new Thurso High School on 15th October, 1958. The influx of Dounreay staff to Thurso created a sudden demand for new facilities and new housing. The high school was built in 1957-58, to a design by Sir Basil Spence who went on to build Coventry Cathedral.

The beach and esplanade at Thurso in 1949.

A new footbridge over the Thurso River.

Thurso's long history is exemplified by the ruins of Old St. Peter's, a church dating back to the time of the Norse earls in the Middle Ages.

The consruction of the reactor and the associated buildings at Dounreay was a major undertaking. The spherical structure housing the reactor became known as 'the Dome' and was adopted as a symbol of modernity. The local press carried these and other pictures in 1957 as a record of the progress being made.

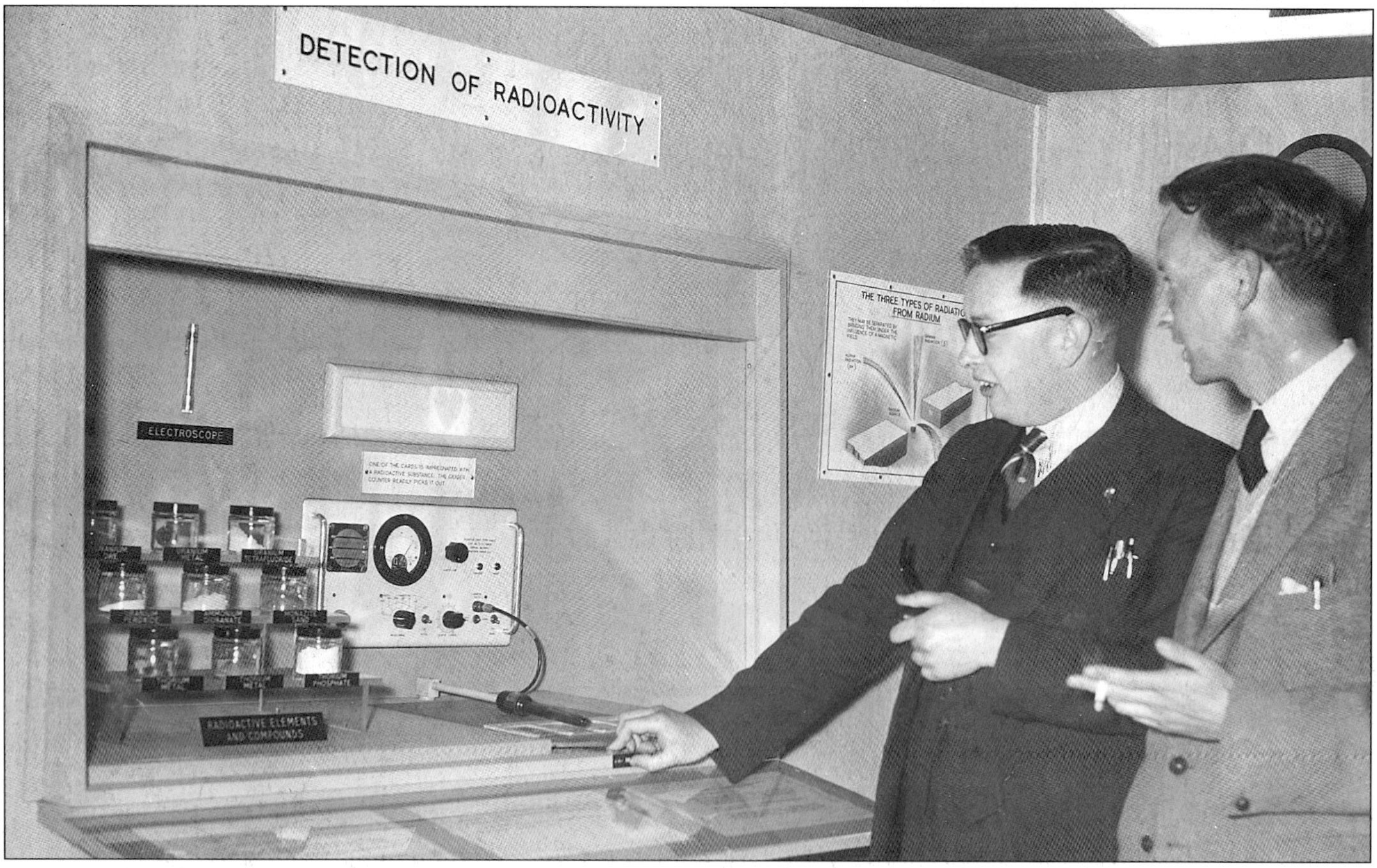

Mr G.B. Wolfinden, the shop manager in the health and safety department of the Atomic Energy Authority, demonstrates the detection of radioactivity on an ace of hearts, in April, 1955.

The low-level effluent tunnel.

What it was all for? Dounreay's fast-breeder reactor was designed to generate cheap electricity and in October, 1962, it became the first plant of its type in the world to achieve this aim. The dial shows the output – 3 megawatts.

The heart of the beast – working on the top of the heavy-water reactor.

Dounreay apprentices getting ready for a coach trip to the Scottish Industries Exhibition, in September, 1959. *(UKAEA copyright)*

Other Industries

In 1956, the Admiralty leased part of the Dounreay site from UKAEA for its Reactor Test Establishment (ARTE) for research on nuclear submarine propulsion. ARTE was re-named HMS *Vulcan* in 1970. Special machinery arrived by rail and sea, such as this 19-ton piece pictured at Thurso station on 4th September, 1961.

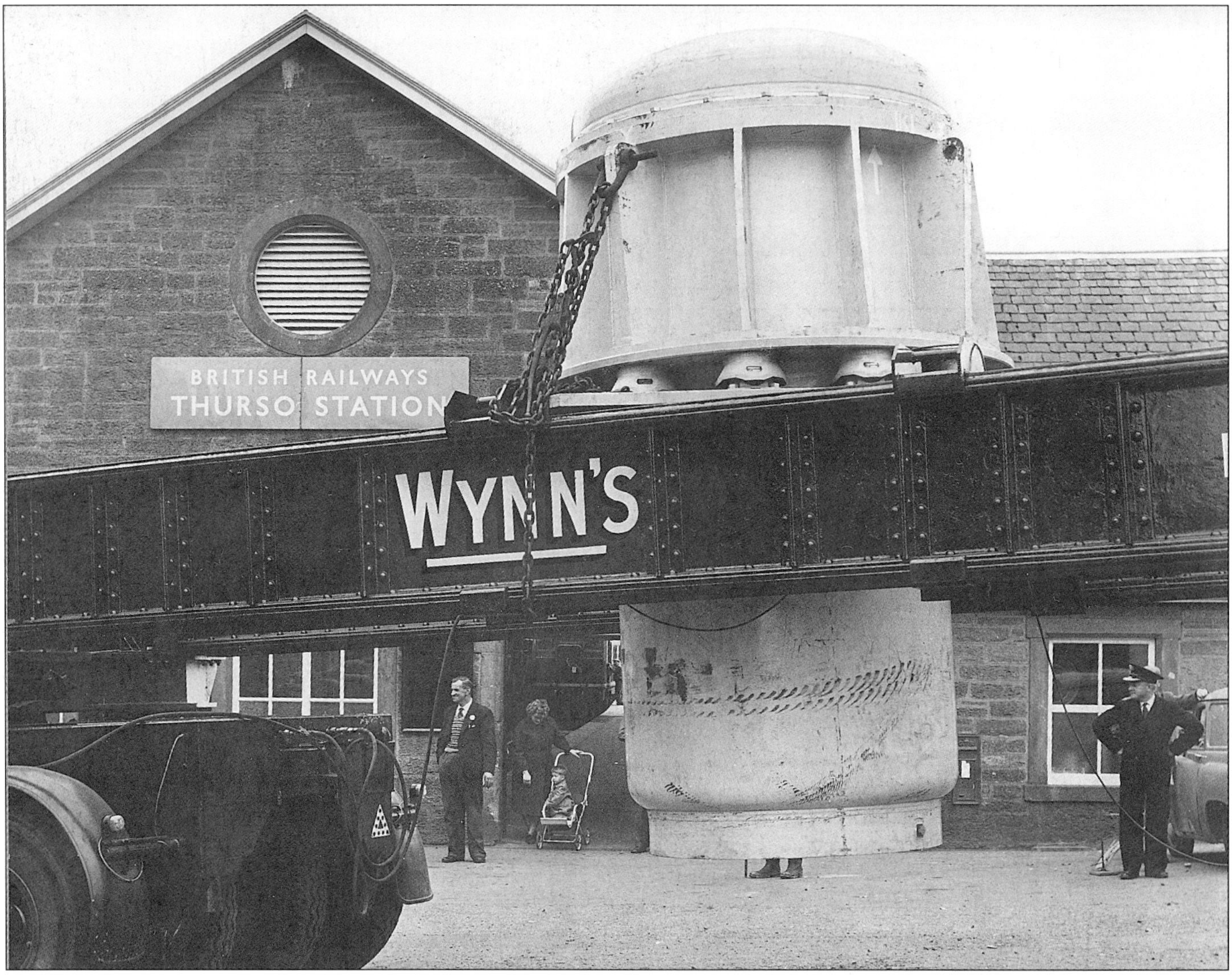

Provost Sutherland, Thurso, with Admiral A.R. Hezlet, Flag Officer Scotland and Northern Ireland, at the opening of Scapa House, as accommodation for Navy personnel, on Monday, 4th March, 1963.

This mysteriously shrouded equipment arrived in Wick for HMS Vulcan on the *Pool Fisher* in March, 1961.

General Election 1955

Sir David Robertson, the Independent Conservative MP for Caithness and Sutherland, played an important role in securing the Dounreay plant for Caithness. In the 1955 General Election he was therefore well placed to fight off the challange from the Labour candidate, Hugh F. Sutherland, seen here canvassing among the Wick railway workers and the Liberal candidate, John S. Mowat, making his pitch to some young Wickers, some of whom at least do not look old enough to vote.

Altnabreac Scheme

The North of Scotland Hydro-Electric Board explored various means of electricity generation and in 1954, set up an experimental plant to burn peat at Braehour, three miles from Westerdale.

The picture shows machinery arriving for the plant, with, on the left, James Miller, the farmer at Braehour and J. Venters, a Board engineer.

The Altnabreac scheme stimulated much discussion and humour throughout Caithness. Donald Grant, better known as 'Castlegreen', wrote a popular poem 'Peats for Power', and the citizens of Halkirk put their own spin on the business with this float in the Halkirk Gala in 1955. *(Submitted by Edward Sutherland).*

As part of the water scheme, a dam was built at Achavarn. The level of Loch Calder was raised by 11 feet.

Loch Calder, which became in 1955, the fount of the county's public water.

Mr W.M. Jollans, the resident engineer, welcomes the Queen Mother to the opening of the Hoy pumping station on 30th April, 1955. Here the water from Loch Calder was filtered and pumped onward to high reservoirs at Stemster Hill, Nybster, Brabstermire and Cnoc Dubh in Latheron. A reservoir at Ormlie was to serve Thurso.

Two views of the brickworks at Thurso East in 1976. *(Submitted by Iain Rennie)*

Transport

Modern transport in the early 1900s – at Pennyland Farm, Thurso. *(Submitted by Finella MacKinnon)*

Donald Begg preparing to board the train at Thurso station to attend the Wool Fair in Inverness, in July, 1930. Donald was one of five brothers, all noted for their farming in the Thurso-Murkle area. *(Submitted by Finella MacKinnon).*

For long the railway was the easiest way to make the long land journey south. Here, in March, 1958, James McIntosh, the signalman at Wick station, receives the 'token' – the device that ensured only one train was on the single-track line at one time, from James Gunn, fireman on the 10.40 from Inverness.

Cars parked at Pennyland during a sale in 1943. Across the road can be seen the wartime Nissen huts for the service personnel. *(Submitted by Finella MacKinnon).*

The long bends at the Ord and the braes at Berriedale were still a serious obstacle to motor traffic at the start of the 1950s. A normal road journey to Inverness could take five hours.

The four men who drove a 90-ton cylindrical steel container 600 miles from Dudley, Worcester, to Dounreay in April, 1956.

The heavy loads of equipment coming north to Dounreay put a strain on the road system. In September, 1956, two Bailey bridges were installed at Berriedale to strengthen the existing river crossings. To allow the work to be completed quickly, the A9 between Helmsdale and Wick was closed from midnight on Wednesday, 26th until the morning of Friday, 28th September. The road crew worked non-stop for 36 hours to complete the task.

Not all the big loads were Dounreay-bound. These fermenting vessels, each 5.5 tons in weight, were destined for the Pulteney Distillery in September, 1960.

Photograph taken behind Station Hotel, Thurso. Mr Sam Mackay, third from right. *(Submittted by S.E. Mackay).*

Mr John Mackay, chauffeur to Dr Elliott, Wick. Photograph taken at John O'Groat's Hotel. 1905 Argyll - Motor.
(Submitted by S.E. Mackay).

Alex Durrand, Stevie's brother Bobby Cormack and Stevie Durrand.
(Submitted by Mrs I. Ferrier)

Stevie Durrand and James Davidson, Town Hall Square, Thurso. *(Submitted by Mrs I. Ferrier).*

Local Progress

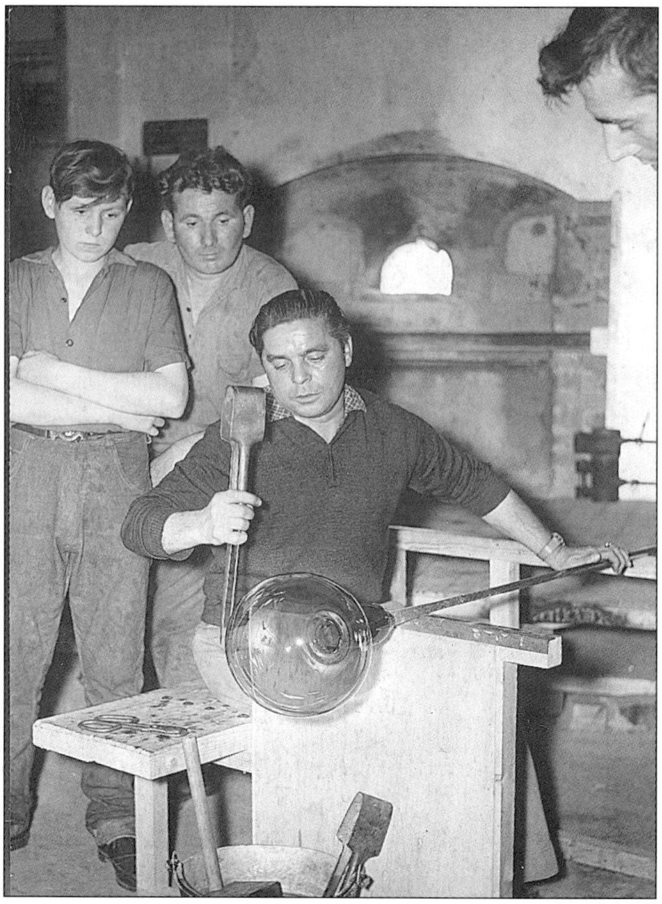

Caithness Glass introduced a new industry to Caithness with the opening of their factory in Wick in October, 1961, an industry that introduced the name of the county to a worldwide audience.
Pictured below on extreme right, are two of the Italian glassblowers who passed on their skills to the local workforce.
Among those pictured are a youthful Willie Byrne, Stanley MacNab and Johnnie Christie.

Improvements to the Berriedale bridges in April, 1963.

Provost William Dunnett and colleagues mark the opening of Wick's one-thousandth council house in January, 1962. The tenants were Mr and Mrs G. Gunn.

In January, 1965, Provost William Dunnett opened Scotland's only gas-heated show-house in Loch Street, Wick.

John Adams probably took this shot of a snowy riverside in the early 1960s. The gasworks and yards beside the harbour bridge at Wick are now gone, their place taken by the medical centre and the swimming pool.

Television arrived in Caithness in the mid-1950s. In June, 1960 the BBC opened a new transmitting station at Thrumster.

Henry Rosie, Aline Mowat, Jess Campbell and Dr Fred Robertson made up the Wick team in the BBC Scotland inter-burgh quiz competition, 'Quizburgh', broadcast on Tuesday, 9th July, 1968. Wick made it to the final to confront Paisley but were beaten 105 points to 90, after a closely fought contest.

Dounreay Visitors

Dounreay's success as a fast-breeder reactor establishment brought visitors to Caithness from all over the world.

Dr Robert Hurst, Dounreay director, (right), greets three scientists from the Soviet Union's fast-reactor team with their interpreter at Wick airport in January, 1960.

A large team from the United States Joint Congressional Committee on Atomic Energy came in 1957.

Dounreay director, Roy Matthews, briefs Michael Noble, Secretary of State in August, 1964.

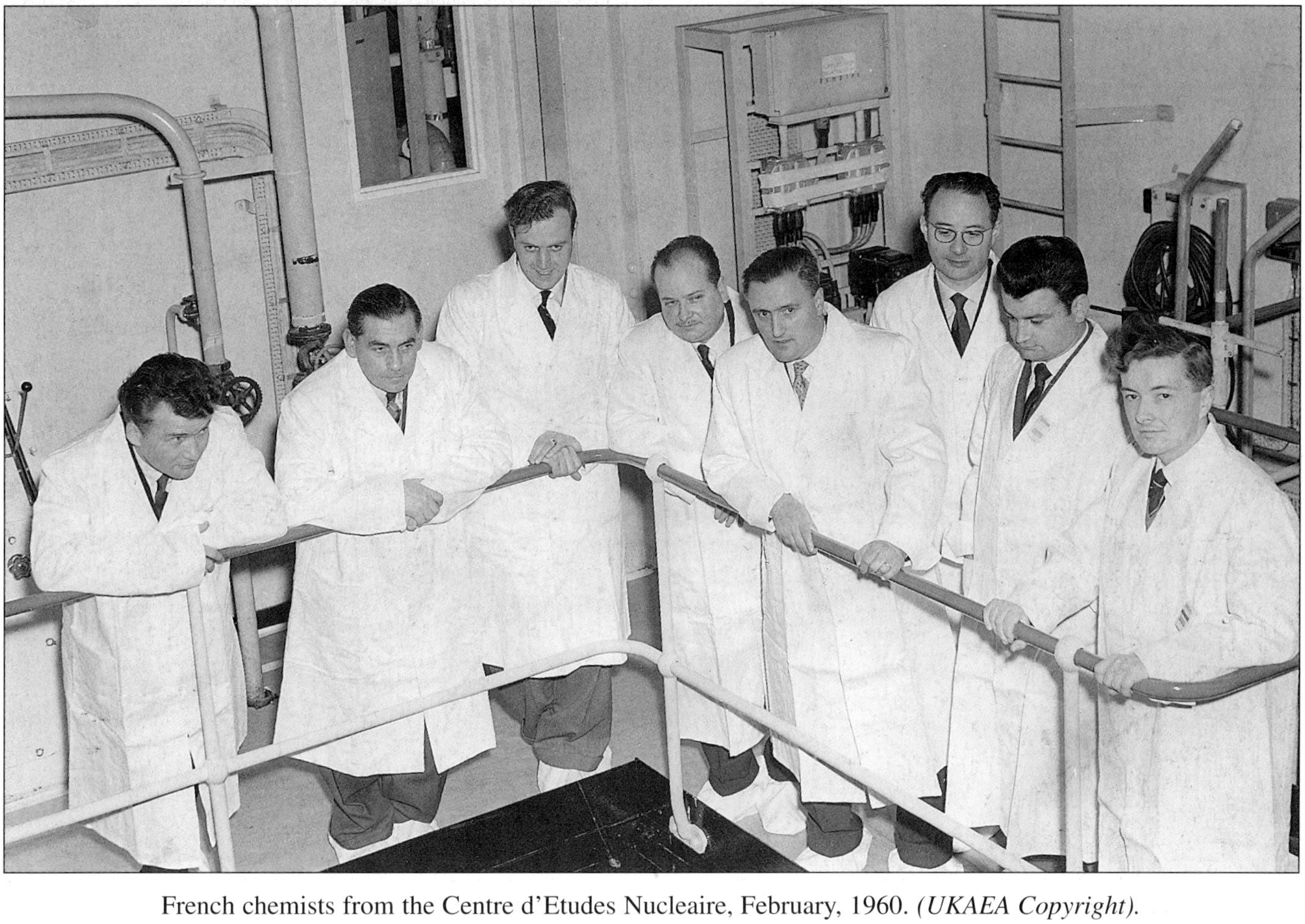

French chemists from the Centre d'Etudes Nucleaire, February, 1960. *(UKAEA Copyright).*

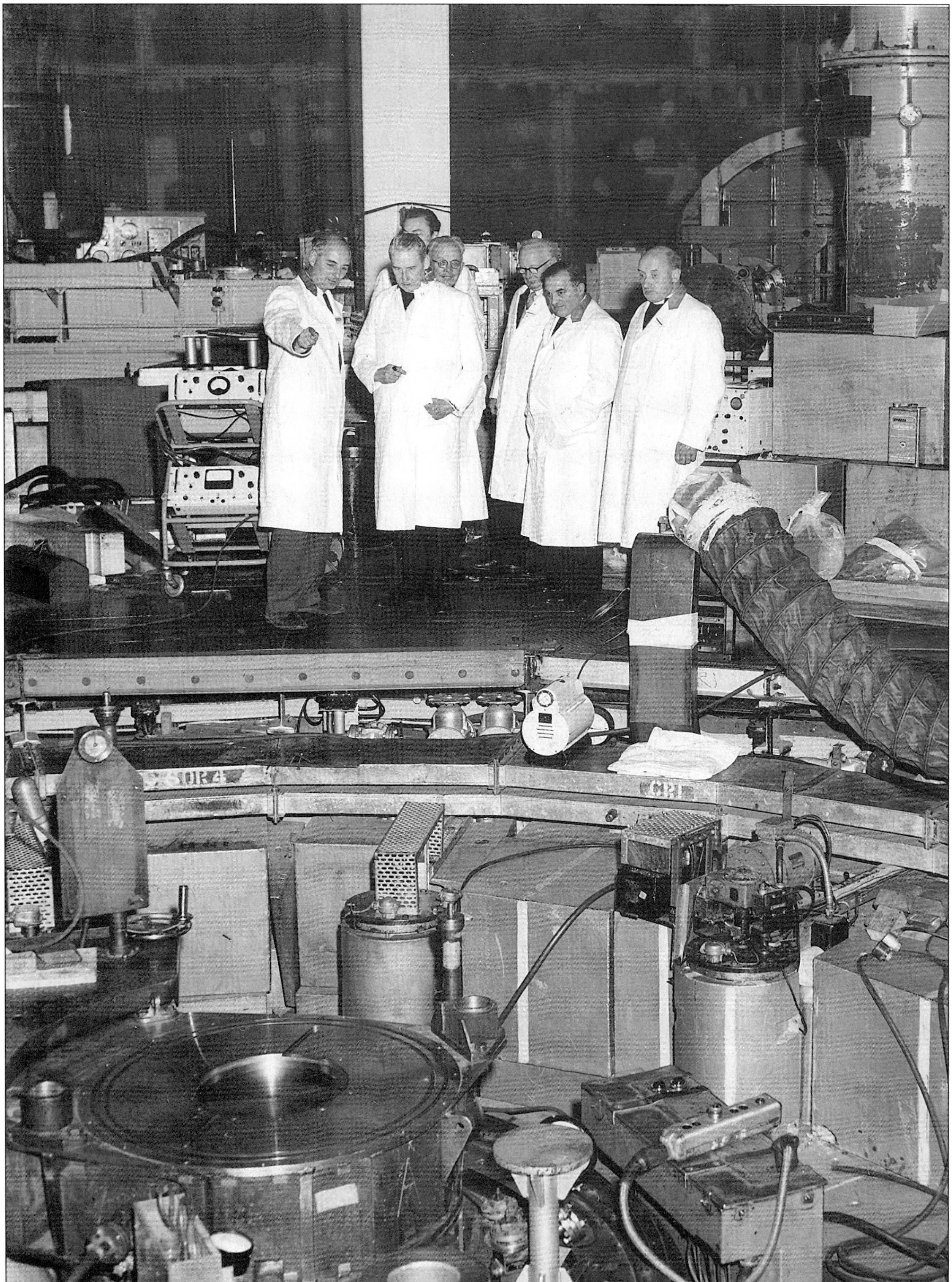

The Right Rev. Dr A. Neville Davidson, Moderator of the General Assembly of the Church of Scotland, came to Dounreay during a ten-day visit to Caithness in September, 1962. *(UKAEA Copyright)*

BBS
BRIDGEND BUILDING SUPPLIES LTD
Specialists in TIMBER FRAMED HOMES, TIMBER, BUILDING MATERIALS & D.I.Y.
TOOLS, POWER TOOLS, LIGHTING, GARDENING SUPPLIES & FURNITURE
Regular SPECIAL OFFERS on a huge range of Household Products
BRIDGEND BUILDING SUPPLIES
BRIDGEND, THURSO
Tel. 01847 892494
Also at
HOMECARE
2 Ulbster Place, Thurso, KW14 8PR
Tel. 01847 896761 or 01847 893894

HIGHLANDER HIGH PERFORMANCE
WINDOWS, DOORS & CONSERVATORIES
With Energy Efficient Warm Edge Technology
Manufactured from high impact PVCu in white, rosewood and cherrywood finishes and fully reinforced. Security glazed and fitted with multi-point locking.
Manufactured in Caithness in a variety of styles and to any size. Fitted throughout the Highlands. Dedicated teamwork by highly skilled and trained technicians.
For FREE professional advice, survey and quotation, from the oldest window company in the county, contact:
VEKA
Approved Fabricator and Installer
norscot
Showroom: Bower Workshops ~ Bower ~ Caithness
Open: Mon. ~ Sat., 10am ~ 2pm. Ample parking.
TELEPHONE: 01955 641303
CPA
Consumer Protection Association
Insurance Backed Guarantee

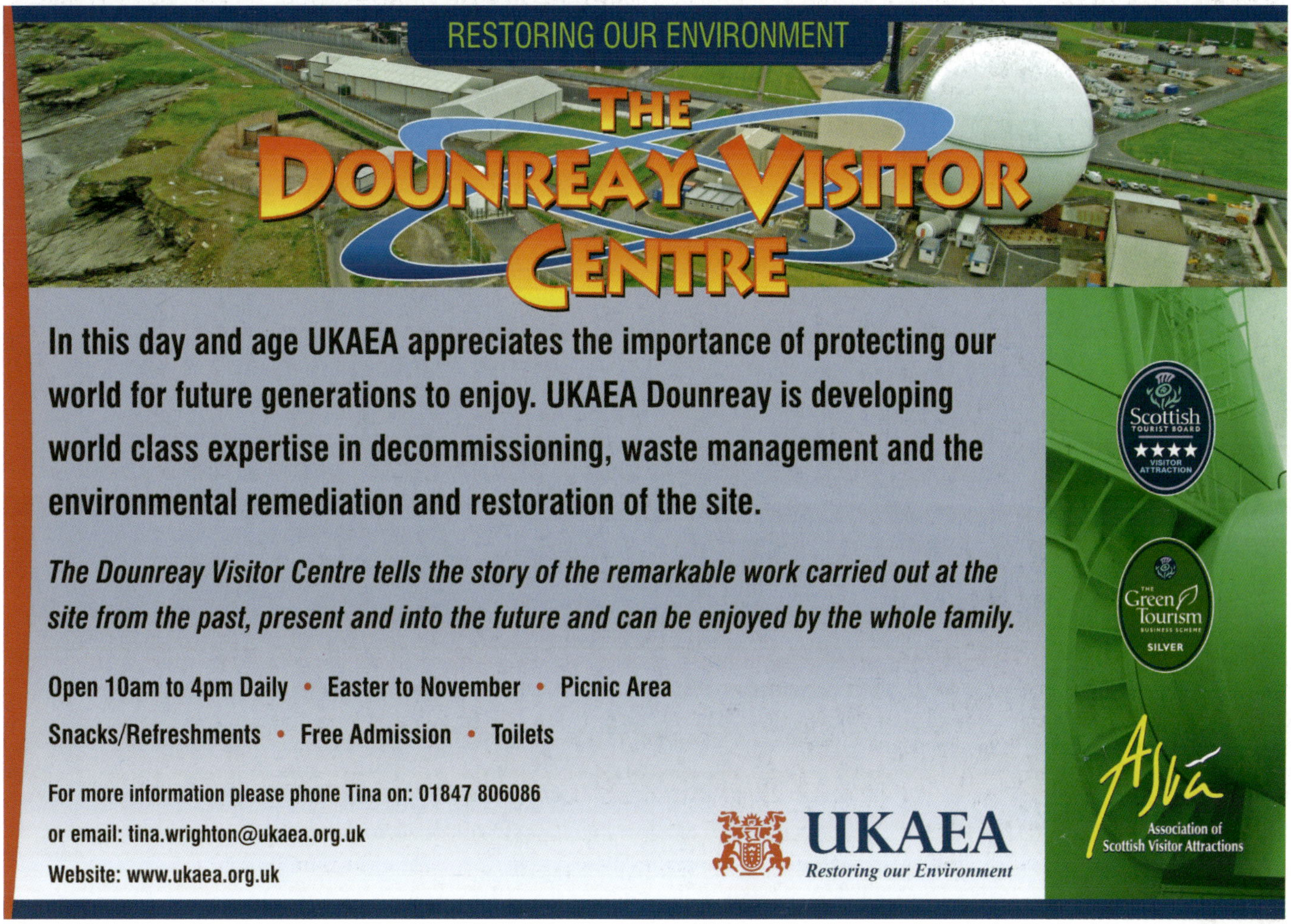
RESTORING OUR ENVIRONMENT
THE DOUNREAY VISITOR CENTRE
In this day and age UKAEA appreciates the importance of protecting our world for future generations to enjoy. UKAEA Dounreay is developing world class expertise in decommissioning, waste management and the environmental remediation and restoration of the site.
The Dounreay Visitor Centre tells the story of the remarkable work carried out at the site from the past, present and into the future and can be enjoyed by the whole family.
Open 10am to 4pm Daily • Easter to November • Picnic Area
Snacks/Refreshments • Free Admission • Toilets
For more information please phone Tina on: 01847 806086
or email: tina.wrighton@ukaea.org.uk
Website: www.ukaea.org.uk
UKAEA
Restoring our Environment
Scottish Tourist Board
Visitor Attraction
Green Tourism Business Scheme
SILVER
Asva
Association of Scottish Visitor Attractions

"Where did you buy it?"
WOULD YOU BELIEVE IT?
ONE LOOK AT RIVERSIDE REPLICAS AND YOU'D EXPECT OUR INTERIOR TO HOUSE LOVINGLY CRAFTED, TRADITIONAL ITEMS, AND YOU'D BE RIGHT. BUT IT'S ALSO HOME TO SOME OF THE MOST CONTEMPORARY NAMES IN INTERIOR DESIGN. OUR RANGES ARE TRULY DIVERSE. BUT TO EXPERIENCE IT, YOU NEED TO STEP INSIDE. YOU'LL SOON QUESTION WHY YOU NEVER THOUGHT OF US BEFORE
Riverside Replicas
RIVERSIDE ROAD, THURSO
TEL: 01847 893553. FAX: 01847 896381
www.riversidereplicas.co.uk

D. Steven & Son
UK & Europe
"Serving Caithness Since 1920"
Daily services to Aberdeen, Peterhead, Glasgow, Newhaven & English and Continental Markets
GENERAL HAULAGE CONTRACTORS & TEMPERATURE CONTROLLED SPECIALISTS
"Scottish European Haulier of the Year, 2004"
Depots at:
Scrabster & Wick (01847) 893070
Aberdeen (01224) 898999
Glasgow (01698) 843313
email: traffic@dsteven–son.co.uk

McAllans
HIGHLANDWEAR SPECIALISTS
WICK + THURSO
Clan Crest Gift Sets
123 Clans available
OUTFITS FOR ALL OCCASIONS
Clan Crest Sporrans
Superior Quality
Culloden Shirts
Available in many colours and styles
ALL OUR PRODUCTS ARE MADE IN SCOTLAND FOR THE HIGHEST QUALITY ASSURED
WWW.MCALLANS.CO.UK
WICK 01955 602547 THURSO 01847 893993

The Royal Connection

The accession to the British throne of Her Majesty Queen Elizabeth is proclaimed at Wick on Saturday, 9th February, 1952. *(Photograph taken by W. Glander and submitted by Maurice Harrington).*

In the summer of 1952, the recently widowed Queen Elizabeth the Queen Mother was staying with her friends, the Vyners, at the House of the Northern Gate in Dunnet and saw on a drive that Barrogill Castle in Mey was for sale. The Queen Mother bought the Castle and began its restoration as a summer residence, renaming it the Castle of Mey.
The Queen Mother with minister, Rev. A.A.M. Gordon, leaves Dunnet Church after attending a Sunday service there in 1952.

The Queen Mother frequently shopped in Thurso.

Vice-Lieutenant Brigadier Sir Keith Murray greeted the Queen Mother when she paid a visit to Dounreay in August, 1961.

The Queen Mother views some of the works at the annual show by the Society of Caithness Artists with Society president, Major J.B. Simpson (left) and Sheriff D.B. Keith, in August, 1963.

Her Majesty Queen Elizabeth on a visit to Caithness in 1964.

The land

Agriculture – the older way. Building a scroo of corn at Brims Castle farm in around 1909. Tractors took the place of horses from the late 1940s but these methods of harvesting remained in use until displaced by the advent of the combine harvester in the 1960s and '70s. *(Submitted by Finella MacKinnon).*

Large farms needed several pairs of horses to work the land. These two Clydesdales were part of the contingent at West Murkle in 1931. *(Submitted by Mrs Catherine Begg).*

These two sheep clipping gangs have taken time out to have their photos taken – at Brims in possibly the 1920s and at Pennyland in 1930. *(Submitted by Finella MacKinnon).*

The staff of the Pennyland dairy, 1933.
(Submitted by Finella MacKinnon).

An auction sale of horses in the Pennyland square, May, 1943.
(Submitted by Finella MacKinnon).

The Caithness parks have produced many prize-winning animals, such as this gimmer from D.C. Macadie, Westfield, which won its class at the County Show in August, 1953.

This cockerel won top place in the Light Sussex class at the same event.

The champion Aberdeen Angus from Noss Farm and his 6-month-old son, who won reserve and the trophy for best Aberdeen-Angus bull bred in Caithness, at the County Show in July, 1956.

The sheep-clipping gang at Houstry in around 1957. *(Submitted by Linda Munro).*

A dramatic moment in the pony race at the County Show, 1958.

John Adams did not identify where he took this picture, during the lambing time, April, 1961.

One of Jim Henderson's ewes at Dunnet Post Office had quads in April, 1962.

Brigadier Sir Keith Murray presents John G. Munro, shepherd for 32 years at West Durran, with a long-service medal, at the annual dinner of the Caithness Agricultural Society in the Portland Arms, Lybster, on 23rd November, 1962.

The County Show in Wick on 4th August, 1962, took place on a very wet day, although these cattle and their handlers seem unperturbed by the conditions.

Margaret Mackay, Halkirk, was chosen as Show Queen at the County Show in August, 1963.
Her attendants were Judith Miller, Dunnet and Nancy Nicolson, Newton.

The Queen Mother encouraged the breeding of a pedigree Aberdeen-Angus herd at her farm of Long-goe.
The *Groat* published this picture on 20th November, 1964.

Members of the Young Farmers Club at Lybster Junior Secondary School visited Clyth Mains, in May, 1965.

Some pupils from Wick High School learn some soil science on a visit to North Killimster farm in April, 1964.

West Murkle – Mr A. Manson pictured with his prize Clydesdale, circa 1931. *(Submitted by Sandy Manson).*

A free copy of *'Caithness a Peek into the Past'* awaits the first reader who can identify the location of this telephone box, together with the name of the farmer.

The Sea

In 1948, Wick was home port to 192 boats of various sizes and Thurso had a fleet of 29, employing all told over five hundred men.

The first lighthouse keepers at the new lighthouse at Strathy Point, in September, 1958.

Noss Head lighthouse.

A sailing vessel docked in Reay harbour in the early 1900s. The empty carts suggest that the cargo has not yet been off-loaded. *(Submitted by Finella MacKinnon).*

Traditional yawls beached at Brims in 1909, within a stone's throw of the farm stackyard. *(Submitted by Finella MacKinnon).*

John Adams took many pictures of incidents at sea, and seems to have been always ready to rush with his camera to the harbour.

On 18th September, 1953, a Grimsby trawler, *Hassett*, was driven ashore at Auckengill. Five of the crew were lost. These are some of the fifteen survivors at the Seamen's Mission in Wick. For their sterling rescue work, the Wick Life-Saving Apparatus Company won an award from the Ministry of Transport.

The trawler, *Jean Stephen,* went ashore at Reiss in January, 1958. The crew are seen here in the Seamen's Mission.

The trawler, *Reggio,* went ashore on Rora Head, Orkney, on 6th November, 1955, but was able to break-free and reach Scrabster under her own power, where these pictures of her arrival were taken. The inquiry into the incident was later reported in the *Groat* on 13th April, 1956.

When the cargo steamer, *Sound Fisher,* sank four miles south-east of Wick on 13th January, 1957, some of the crew were taken care of in the Seamen's Mission, while others were tended in Bignold Hospital. Nurse Sheila Mackay from Keiss with Second Officer Alfred Hart and Seaman John Hallewell.

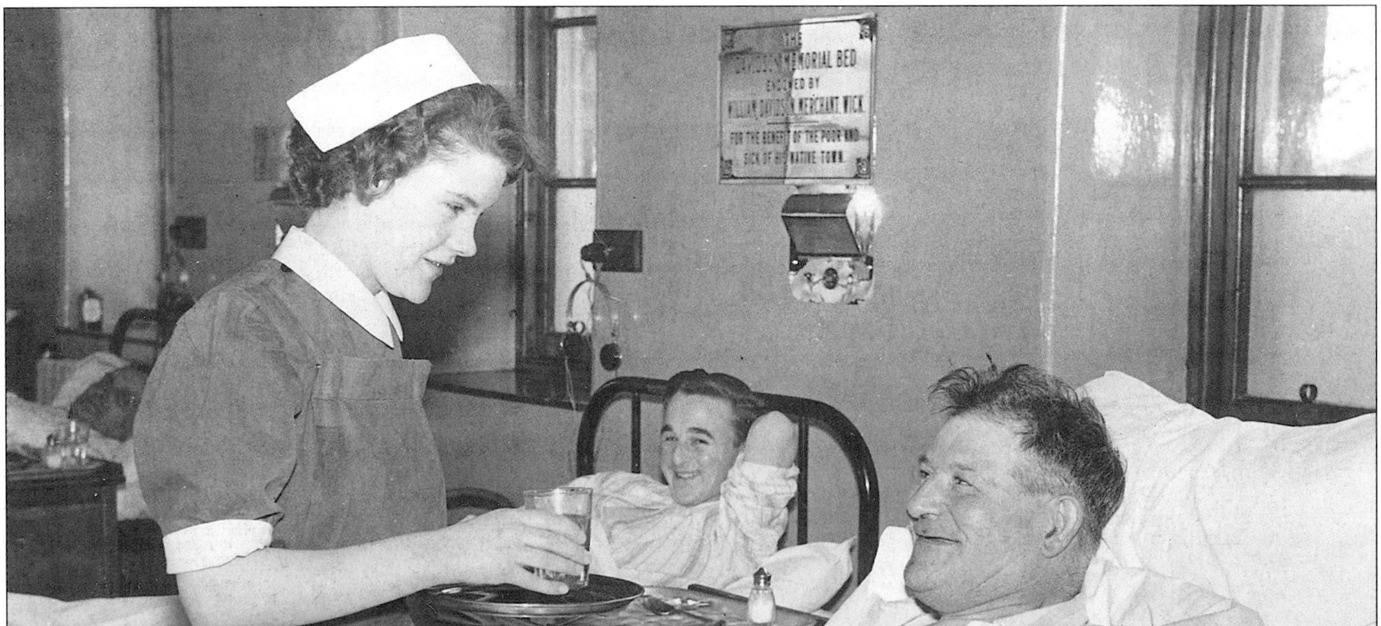

The Queen Mother is introduced to Coxwain Angus Mackintosh and his crew during Lifeboat Week in Scrabster, in August, 1962.

The Spray tows the *Ajax* into harbour after the latter developed engine trouble in September, 1964.

Right - The *Boy Peter* skipper, James Sutherland, had her wheelhouse damaged in a collision in fog with an unidentified vessel - possibly Russian - to the west of the Pentland Firth on 29th August, 1968.
The *Boy Peter's* skipper and crew were unhurt.
Left - On 10th July, 1965 a Polish herring vessel sought refuge after she had collided in darkness with another unknown vessel 70 miles east of Wick. John Adams photographed the smashed wheelhouse and gunwale.

One of the most unusual maritime incidents of the period involved the Wick seiner, *Enterprise*. The *Enterprise* (skipper George Swanson) found a Norwegian boat *Juny* deserted and drifting off Orkney in early June, 1965. The *Enterprise* towed the abandoned vessel into Wick. It turned out that the Norwegian fishermen had abandoned the *Juny*, thinking she would sink, after she had been disabled in a storm on 4th May. She stayed afloat however, and drifted across the North Sea. John Adams photographed skipper, Jens Klevens (with cap) of the Norwegian boat *Sylvana* and his crew when they came to Wick on 25th June to tow the errant *Juny* home.

An important aspect of Wick's maritime connection was the presence of the Wick Radio Station, a vital link in the communication network covering the northern seas. The new transmitters installed in 1952 made the Wick station one of the best equipped in the world. Ernest Marples, postmaster general, visited the station in July, 1958.

Schooldays through the ages

The Higher English class at the Miller Institution (later Miller Academy) in 1900. Obviously all-female interest. *(Submitted by Finella MacKinnon).*

Miss Mary Sinclair's class at Halkirk in around 1945. *(Submitted by D. Campbell).*

Watten School in 1948. *(Submitted by Jean MacDonald).*

The pupils of Spittal School in 1950-51 with their teacher, Miss Macintosh. *(Submitted by D. Campbell, Thurso)*

A sad aspect of rural life in the 1950s and '60s was the closure of several of the smaller schools as rolls fell and the costs of education rose. Spittal School closed in 1970, the last of the small schools in Halkirk parish to go, having been preceded by Banniskirk and Harpsdale (1953), Westerdale (1957) and Scotscalder (1962). In the towns and larger villages, however, there was a need for more and better schools.

The members of this Infant class in West Public School, Thurso, won a cup for song and dance in the 1956 Music Festival. *(Submitted by Mrs Mennie)*

William Sinclair, the managing director for Scotland for the Dunlop Rubber Company, was guest of honour at the opening of the new junior secondary school in Halkirk, in November, 1956. Mr Sinclair was the brother of the well-known Rev. R.R. Sinclair.

Wick North School, 1962. *(Maurice Harrington).*

The Old South School, Pulteney, being demolished in 1964. It stood on the corner of Macrae and Kinnaird Streets.

Wick High pupils off to France in 1965.

Commercial class at Wick High School in 1955. *(Submitted by D. Manson).*

North School, Wick, 1950s. *(Submitted by D. Manson)*

Pulteneytown Academy, circa 1890s. *(Submitted by D. Manson)*.

West Watten School, 1936. *(Submitted by Jean Macdonald).*

Class of eight, Watten School, circa 1939/40. *(Submitted by Jean Macdonald).*

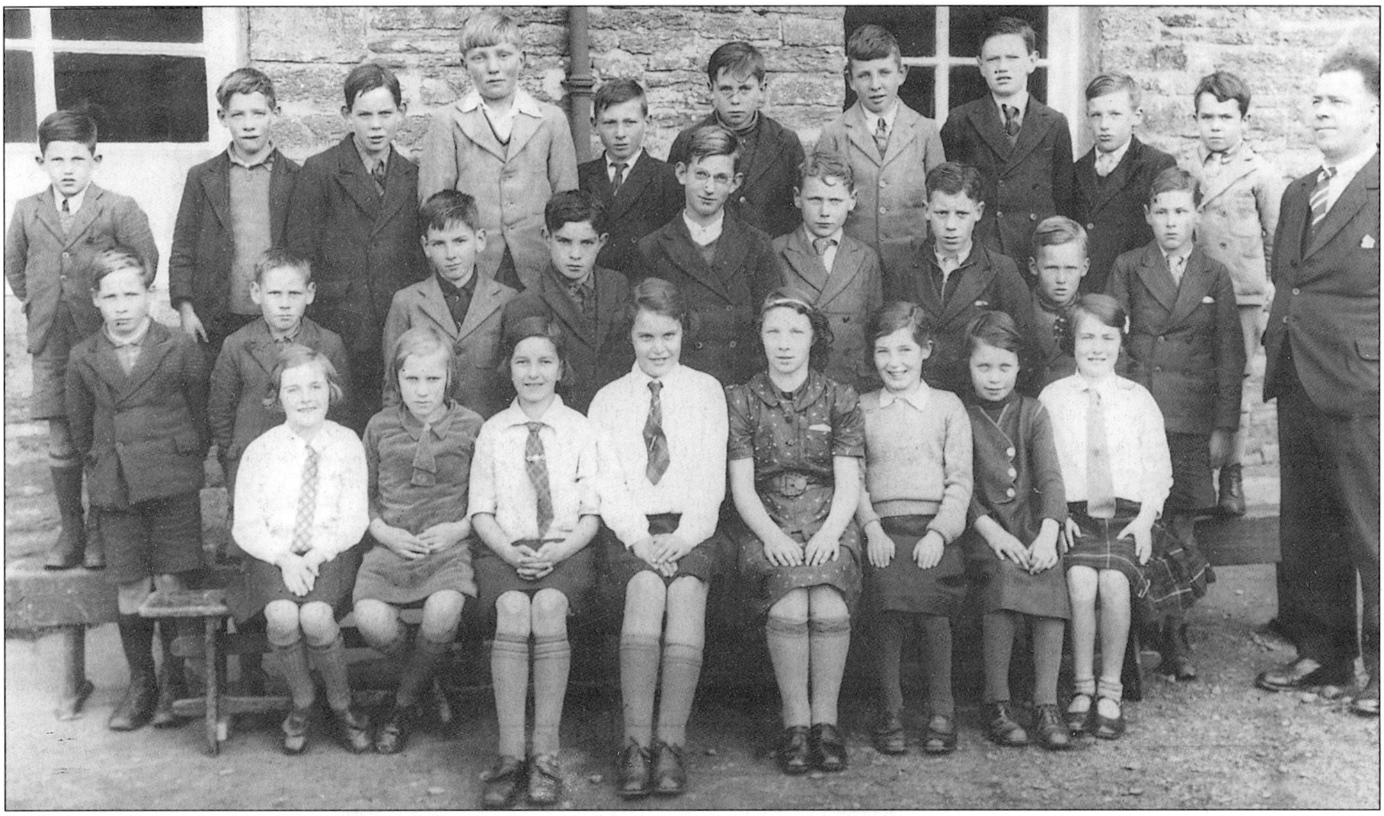

Watten School, 1938. *(Submitted by Jean Macdonald).*

Halkirk Primary School, 1946, *(Submitted by George Forbes).*

Boultach School, Latheronwheel 1933/4.
(Submitted by Mr Macdonald, Watten).

Halkirk School, 1946. *(Submitted by Edward Sutherland).*

The daily round

This selection of pictures, from Adams' work and from other sources, captures a wide range of people and moments.

The 1950s and '60s saw major changes in social life. Some old practices and customs gradually gave way to new ways. John Adams captured a hint of the changes in some of his pictures, while others are examples of the standard fare of a local newspaper.

Some Australian soldiers being entertained at Pennyland at the end of the First World War. *(Submitted by Finella MacKinnon).*

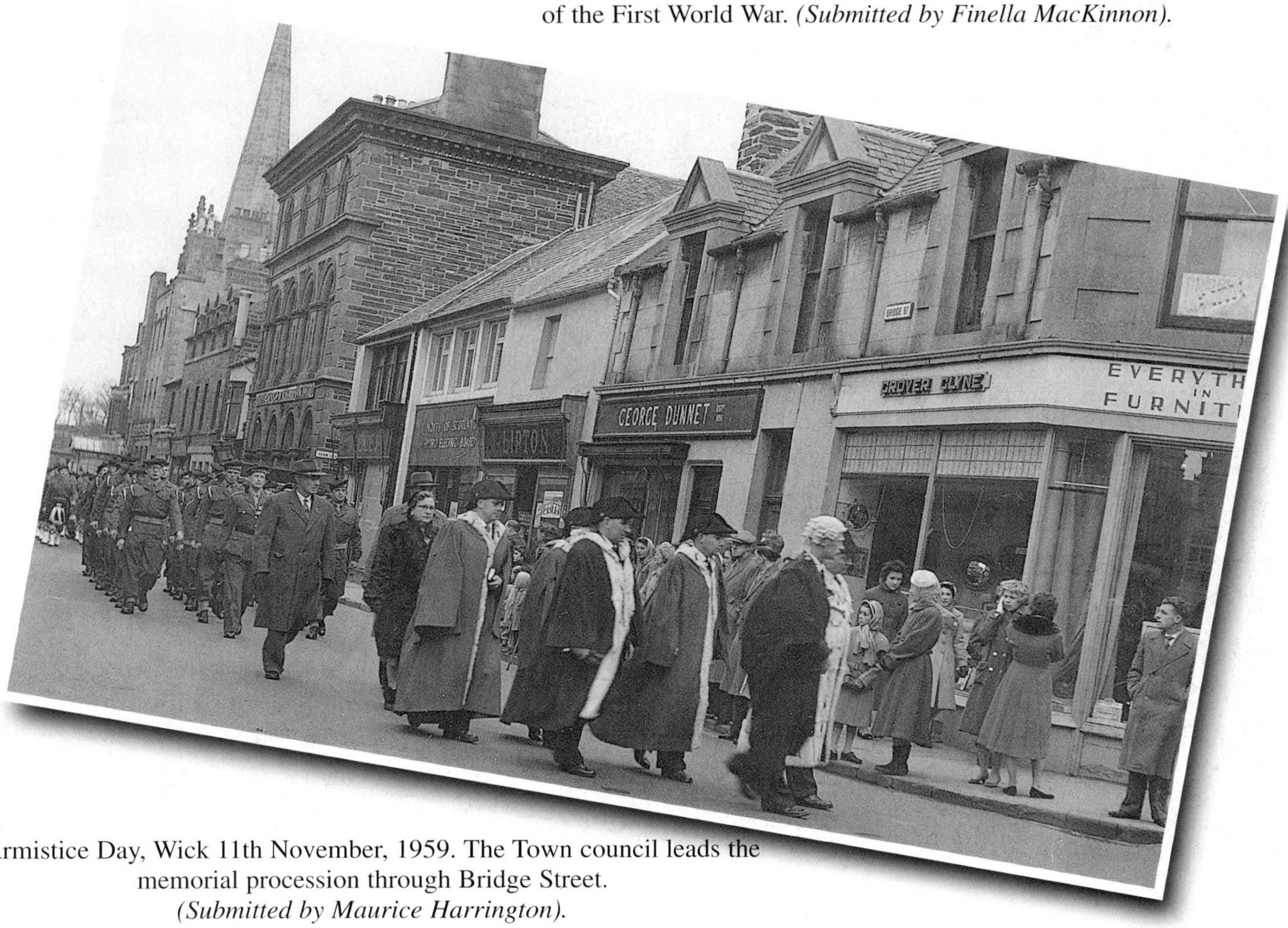

Armistice Day, Wick 11th November, 1959. The Town council leads the memorial procession through Bridge Street. *(Submitted by Maurice Harrington).*

Wick Girls Pipe Band on parade, Armistice Day, November, 1959. *(Submitted by Maurice Harrington).*

Norman Glass, author of "Caithness and the War", is in the centre of this group of the Groat's printing staff in 1964, which also includes Charlie Nicolson (left), Duncan McLean (2nd right) and George Harrold (right). *(Submitted by Maurice Harrington).*

Jamie Cormack with Helen McLaren at Huna, 1950s.
(Submitted by Jamie Cormack Manson).

Santa Claus at the Station Hotel, Wick, 1952.

Chief Constable J.W. Georgeson, with the winners of the safe-driving awards, Mackay's Hotel, Wick, July, 1954.

In this social gathering at Stemster farmhouse in 1956, Mr and Mrs Robert Haig of Auld Petty House, Inverness, are receiving a wedding gift from the tenants of the Stemster and Brabsterdorran estates. Mrs Haig was the daughter of Mrs Henderson of Stemster (seated centre with handbag).

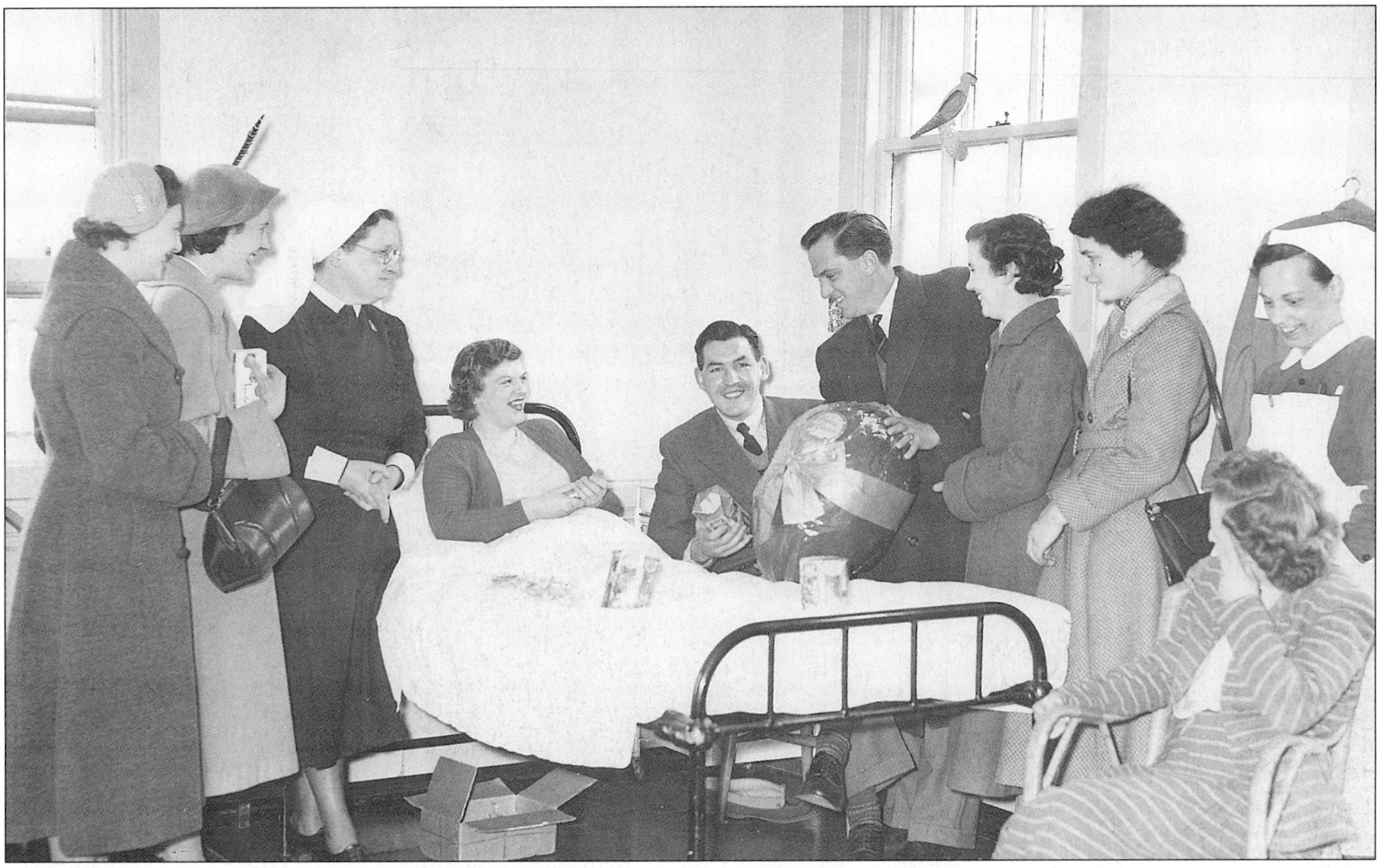

Woolworths presented giant Easter eggs, such as this 14-pound specimen, to the patients in Bignold Hospital in 1955 (pictured here) and in 1956.

Mass tourism was still in the future and in March, 1956, when this picture was taken, a large proportion of the visitors to Caithness were returning exiles. D.W. Ross was a native Wicker who had emigrated to Toronto, and on his return visit he was greeted at Wick airport by Sir David Robertson MP and Lady Robertson.

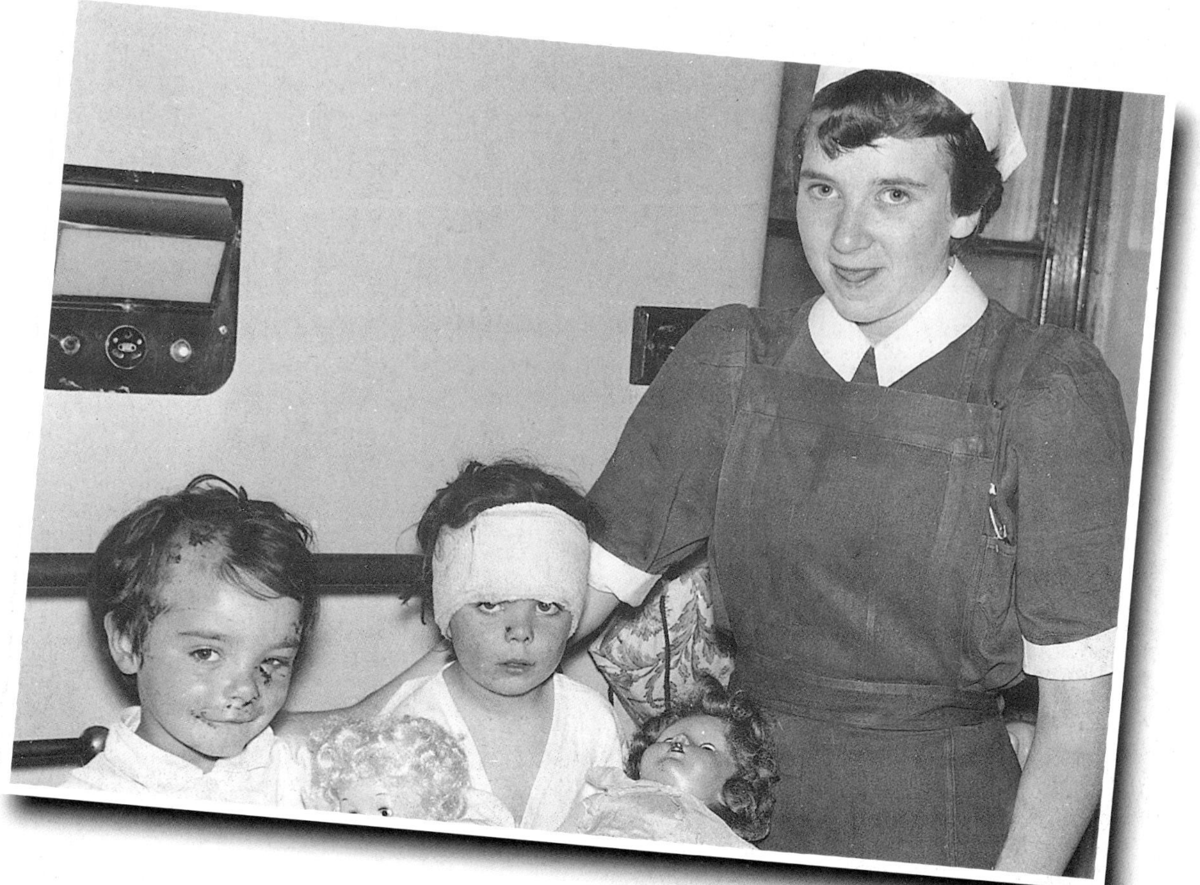

An unusual coincidence brought these sisters, 5-year-old Caroline and 3-year-old Yvonne Sutherland, together in Bignold Hospital in September, 1957. Caroline was bitten by a dog and within 24 hours, Yvonne fell from a car. The *Groat* printed the picture on 13th September.

The Scottish Policewoman's Conference at the Station Hotel, Wick, on 10th October, 1957.

Provost James Leishman switches on the Christmas tree lights outside the Town Hall in Wick, on 20th December, 1958.

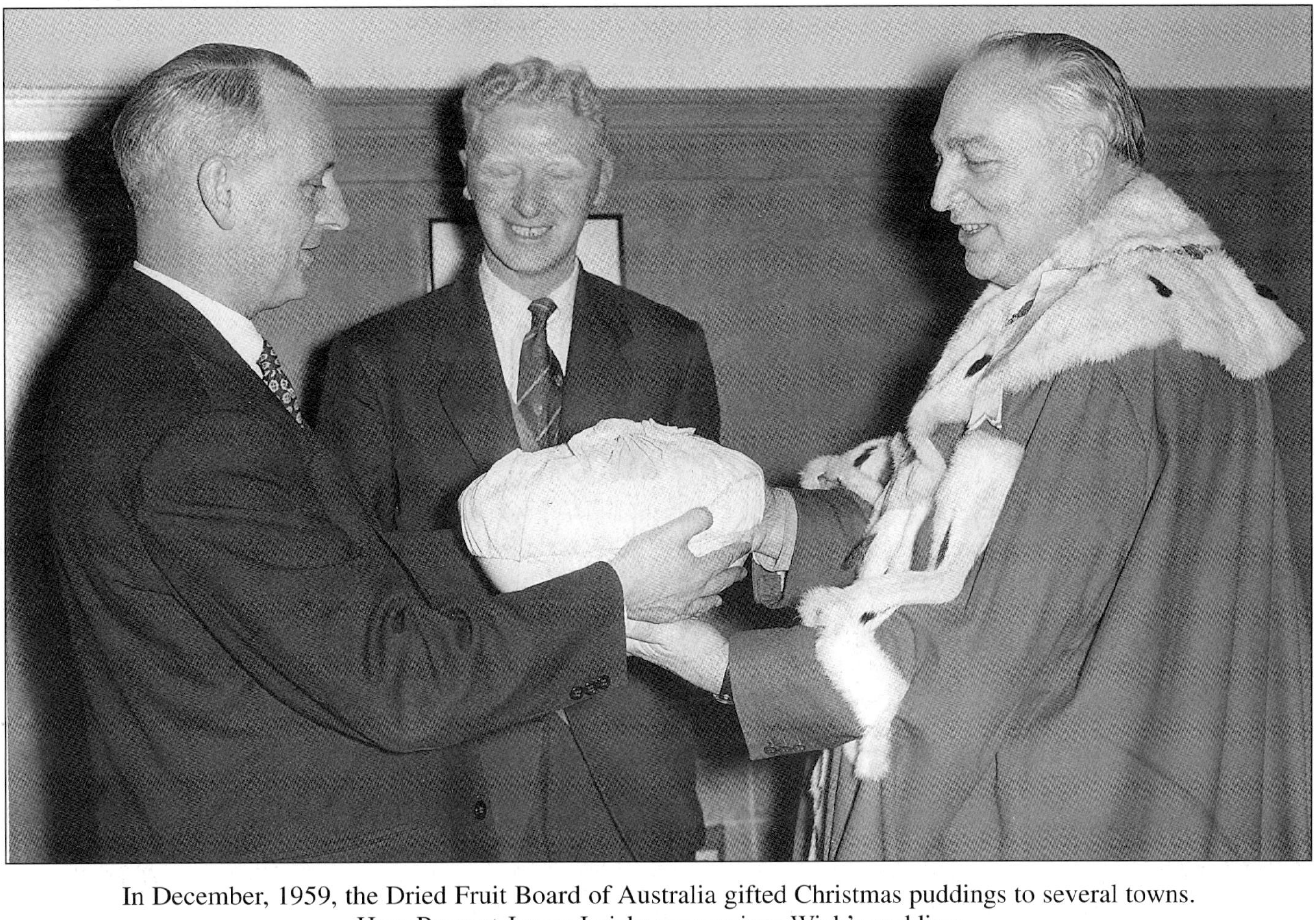

In December, 1959, the Dried Fruit Board of Australia gifted Christmas puddings to several towns. Here Provost James Leishman receives Wick's pudding.

Retiring postman, John Budge, is carried from the Wick sorting office by his colleagues in September, 1959, after 46 years service.

This picture of the staff of the Bignold Hospital was taken probably in the early 1960s.

A mannequin parade in the Rosebank Hotel ballroom in April, 1961.

Mrs Barbara Macleod, Dunbeath, on the occasion of her 100th birthday, with her daughter, Mrs T. Macbeath, her granddaughter, Mrs J. Reeve, and Mrs Reeve's brother, John Macbeath.
The *Groat* printed the picture on 28th April, 1961.

Wedding anniversaries were favourite subjects, then as now.

The diamond wedding of Mr and Mrs John Bremner, 1 Brown Place, Wick.
(*Groat*, 19 December, 1958).

Mr and Mrs John Davidson, 7 Harrow Hill, Wick, taken on the occasion of their diamond wedding.
(*Groat*, 3rd May, 1957).

Two golden weddings: Mr and Mrs James Martin, Seaview Farm, Oldwick and Mr and Mrs George McKain, 20 Wellington Street, Wick. Both were printed in the *Groat*, on 29th December, 1961.

A.E. Rowe in Castletown was surprised in March, 1962 to find a balloon that appeared to have drifted all the way across the Atlantic from New York.

In April, 1962, van driver, Owen Farquhar, 55 Girnigoe Street, Wick, and his 18-year-old assistant, Walter Taylor from Ulbster, saved two mothers and two children from drowning in the river at Lochinver.

Caithness university students staged this coffee morning with stalls in the Station Hotel, Wick, as part of their charities campaign in April, 1964.

The Wick Town Council laid on this old folk's party in February, 1965.

Rev. C.H. Attwater and his bride, Gillian Brown, receive a wedding gift from the congregation of St. Peter and the Holy Rood Episcopal Church, Thurso, in February, 1965.

David Oag, the editor of the *Groat,* presents a record player, a gift from the Toronto Caithness Association, to Forse House, March, 1965.

Robert and Helen Maclennan's wedding in America in 1968.

Pictured here outside his Argyle Square loft with his wife, Mary, Wulldag Miller was famed both for his skill as a master baker and for his successes as a pigeon fancier. *(Submitted by Michael Miller).*

Donnie Mackay with his wife and family in the Ensign Shop, the business he ran for many years in High Street, Wick. *(Photograph: Northern Studios) (Submitted by Thomas Mackay).*

Hamish Webster in his licensed grocery in Louisburgh Street, Wick.
(Photograph: J. McDonald) (Submitted by Thomas Mackay).

The well-known journalist and broadcaster, Jack House, opens the Liberal fair in the Wick Assembly Rooms in 1965.

This picture appeared in the *Groat* under the headline, 'Frogman recovers his own car'. He was Hamish Duncan and he escaped from his skidding car only seconds before it crossed the road at the foot of Harbour Terrace and plunged into the harbour, on the evening of 2nd February, 1969.

A happy group at St. Peter's Manse, Thurso, in the 1920s. *(Submitted by Finella MacKinnon).*

Members of the Thurso Boys Brigade at Pennyland House, the birthplace of the founder of the BB, in around 1930. *(Submitted by Finella MacKinnon).*

HRH The Princess Royal, visited Wick in June, 1949, in her role as president of the Girl Guides. She was greeted by Sir Archibald Sinclair, Lord Lieutenant of the county, and watched a pageant at the riverside.

HRH The Princess Royal greeted by Sir Archibald Sinclair. (see previous page)

Miss H. Munro from Thurso, secretary of the Girl Guides Association, at the mike at a camp-fire event in the grounds of Wick High School on 7th May, 1955.

In March, 1956, the 2nd Wick Troop of the Boy Scouts staged its first variety show in the Kirkhill Scout Hall.

The president of the Boys Brigade visits the Wick group in 1957. *(Submitted by Mervyn Hill).*

The Honorable Robin Sinclair takes the salute at the Scouts' thanksgiving parade on the occasion of Lord Baden Powell's birthday in 1957.

Some Scouts try their paddles at canoeing in the Trinkie, in the 1950s. *(Submitted by D. Manson).*

Wick Army Cadets repair the Kinderspiel footbridge over the Thurso River to raise funds for the Freedom from Hunger Campaign in April, 1963.

An exercise in tent pitching, 1965.

Brownies on a clear-up of Watten in 1979. *(Submitted by J. Macdonald, Watten).*

Mrs M.A. Sinclair is presented with a hymnary by St. Andrew's Church, Pulteneytown in June, 1958.

The Sunday School from Wick Baptist Church on their annual picnic in around 1960.
Outings, always known as 'the picnic', were standard events in the calendar of rural schools and Sunday schools.
(Submitted by Maurice Harrington).

This image of St. Fergus was one of a set of nine new windows in Wick Old Parish Church dedicated on 5th November, 1961.

Thurso Freemasons in the 1920s. (*Submitted by Finella MacKinnon*).

The ladies of the Banniskirk WRI in the 1940s. (*Submitted by J. Campbell, Halkirk*).

The opening of the Halkirk British Legion Hall in 1948. The ceremony was performed by Colonel Palmer, here watched by, among others, Lady Sinclair and Sir Archibald Sinclair. *(Submitted by Edward Sutherland, Halkirk).*

Veterans of the 5th Seaforths hold a reunion in the Pentland Hotel, Thurso, in April, 1956.

The Caithness branch of the Scottish Rock Gardens Club held an outing to a garden at Buckies, near Thurso, May, 1956.

The annual outing of the Wick Baptist Church Women's Guild on 28th June, 1956, included a visit to the Castle of Mey. Ex-bailie, William Dunnett is taking the photo.

John Dawson from Inverness judges the entries in the annual exhibition of floral decorations held by the Wick branch of the British Sailors Society, in June, 1956.

Wick Girls Pipe Band won the Scottish championship in 1958. *(Submitted by D. Manson, Wick).*

The WRI held an annual East of Caithness bulb show - these scenes are from 1957 and 1962.

Three winners at the Caithness Music Festival in 1964 – from left to right, Mrs J.E.A. Bishop, Mrs J. Humphries, and Mrs M. Wilkinson.

James Flett, conductor of Thurso Choral Society, January, 1964.

Moira Anderson joined the Wick Arion Choir, conducted by Aline Mowat, as guest singer in this concert in the Assembly Rooms, in March, 1965.

James Cormack ('Cuba') of Kirkhill put his collection of fans on display at the fundraising sale of the Wick Ladies Lifeboat Guild in September, 1964.

Thurso Townswomen's Guild threw their 35th birthday party in the Royal Hotel, on 7th December, 1965.

Daniel the St. Bernard, who belonged to the Shearer family who ran the Music Shop in Victoria Place, Wick, joined this fundraising drive for the SSPCA in 1966. The humans in the picture are George Henderson, headmaster of Pulteneytown Academy, Jeanette Shearer, Willie Ben Mackay of the SSPCA, and Hugh Stewart, director of education.

On Stage

Before television became widespread in the late 1950s, there was a keen interest in amateur dramatics and many clubs existed throughout the county, often going on tour in the winter months to other districts.

The title of this stage show, by the pupils of the Miller Academy in the 1920s, is unknown.
(Submitted by Finella MacKinnon).

Isobel Lewis plays the queen and Annie Spowart the witch, in this play staged in the Rifle Hall, to raise funds for the North School in 1936.
(Submitted by Mrs Anne Wares, Weydale, Thurso)

Wick Players attracted over 1,200 people over three nights to see their production of *Dear Octopus* at the Rifle Hall on 24th, 25th and 26th March, 1948.

Puss in Boots, the Wick pantomime in the Boys Brigade Hall at Christmas 1952. Hugh Lyall played the cat and Effie Eilkie played Roddy, the miller's son.

The Wick Players won through to the final of the Scottish Community Drama Association final in April, 1958, in Troon, with their production of Molière's *Sganarelle*. *(John O'Groat Journal, 21st March, 1958).*

Thurso Players staged Noel Coward's *Hay Fever* in May, 1958.

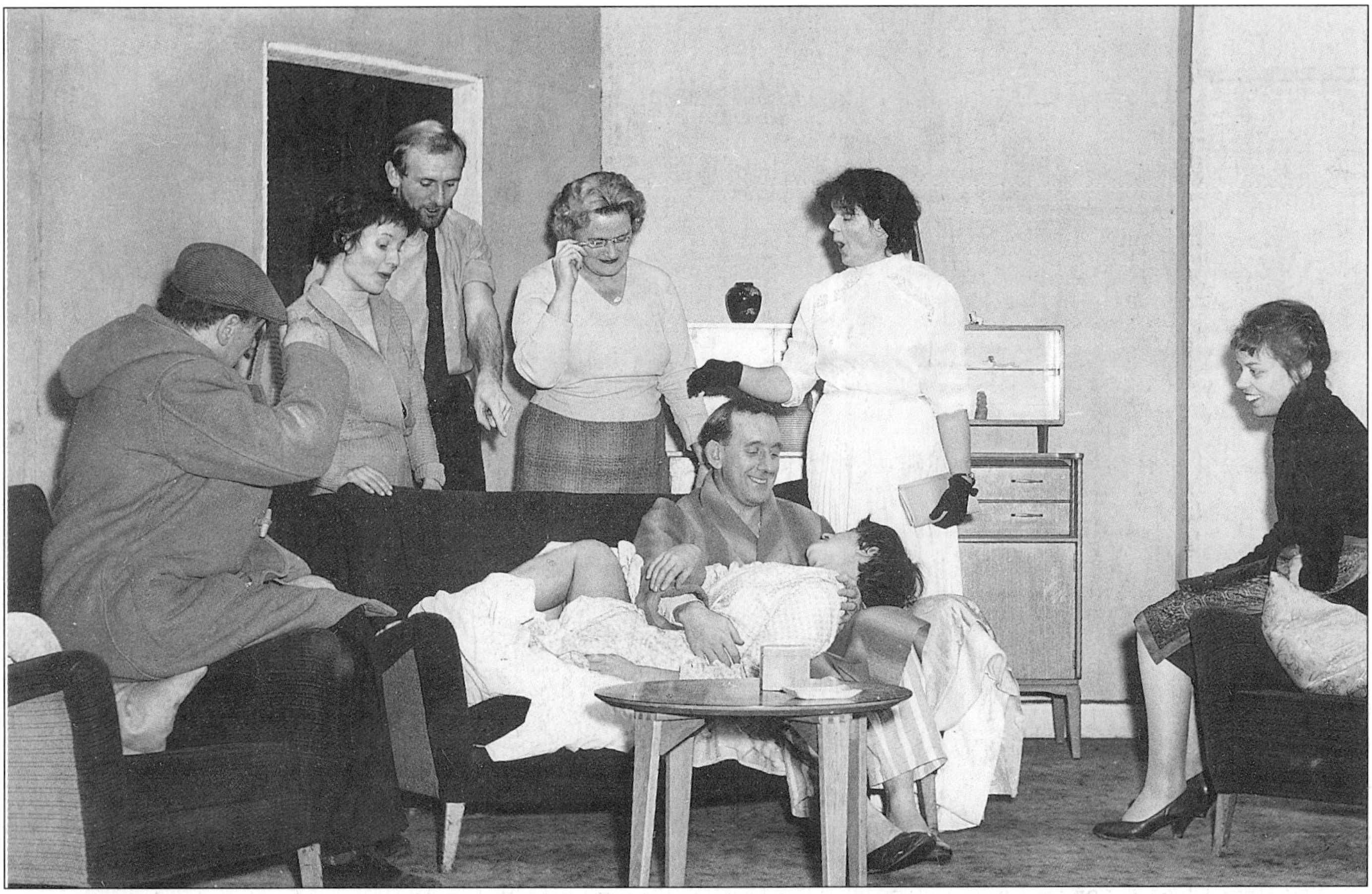

A scene from *Count Your Blessings* by Ronald Jeans, with the Dounreay Drama Group in Thurso Town Hall in November, 1960.

Wick-born actress, Fiona Clyne, in a scene from a television version in October, 1959, of *The Third Man,* with Michael Rennie (right) in the title role.

Mrs J.G. Walford produced this nativity play at the St. Peter and the Holy Rood Episcopal Church in December, 1958.

1968 Gala Fancy Dress Parade. Judges Mrs Mary Clavet (née Hendry) from U.S.A. and her daughter, Katherine.
(Submitted by Mr Maurice Harrington).

Let's dance

The Farmers Ball in Thurso, probably in the Territorial Drill Hall, in the early 1930s. A number of the guests seemed to have blinked together under the effect of the flashgun. (Submitted by Finella MacKinnon).

Another Farmers Ball, a few years later in 1936-37, but in the same venue. *(Submitted by Catherine Begg, Thurso)*

By the 1950s, the farmers and their partners seem to have become much more laid back – the farmers dinner-dance in the Royal Hotel in 1957.

The Farmers dinner dance in the Royal Hotel, 1957.

Highland Bus Ball, 1949. *(Submitted by Catherine Begg, Thurso).*

The RAF Ball, in the Station Hotel, Wick, February, 1959. *(Submitted by Mina and Maurice Harrington).*

The Bankers Ball in the Royal Hotel, Thurso, in the 1960s. *(Submitted by Mina and Maurice Harrington).*

The Rev. George Bell from Canisbay, looks appropriately passionate addressing the haggis at this Burns Supper in 1961, in the Seaview Hotel, John O'Groats. *(Submitted by Mina and Maurice Harrington).*

The 11th Seaforths (TA) annual ball at the Station Hotel, Wick, on Friday, 1st November, 1963. *(Submitted by Mina and Maurice Harrington).*

The Seaview Hotel, John O'Groats, was a popular venue in the early 1960s for dinner-dances. These two pictures capture the happy crowd on separate occasions. *(Submitted by Maurice Harrington).*

The Labour Party Dinner Dance held in the Seaview Hotel, John O'Groats, in the sixties.
(Submitted by Maurice Harrington).

Staff of Woolworths, Wick, line up for the camera in 1954.

Farmers Ball held in the Royal Hotel, Thurso in the sixties. *(Submitted by Maurice Harrington).*

Heather Day collectors in the early 1960s.

A gathering at the Rosebank Playing Fields, Wick, in the early 1960s

The Shore, Wick, 1960/1. *(Submitted by ≈Maurice Harrington).*

Fitted kitchen 60s style, in one of the prefab houses in Loch Street, Wick.

Armistice Day Parade, Wick, November, 1959. *(Submitted by Maurice Harrington).*

Armed Services recruitment drive, held in the Pavilion Cinema, Wick.

Watten Guides, 1967, with Lady Thurso seated in the centre.
(Photograph: J. McDonald) (Submitted by Mrs MacDonald, Watten)

Wick Scouts, 1948. Bert Sutherland, who submitted this photograph, is pictured second left (front row).

Liberal Party Annual Ball, held in the Royal Hotel, Thurso.
Seated (left to right): Margaret and Hugh Cochrane, Mrs Mackie (MP's wife), Will Smith, Maggie Smith, Rita Swanson, unknown. Standing L-R: George Sinclair, Isobel Gunn (Gerston).
Directly in the middle are Dan and Betty Coghill (Skinnet). Directly at the back is the Hon. Robin Sinclair.
(Submitted by James Gunn, Halkirk).

The opening of the British Legion Hall, Sinclair Street, Halkirk, circa 1949.
Back L-R: George Forbes, John Paul, Dod Manson, Hugh Bain, Sandy Gunn, Mr Chalmers, Alan Cormack, Alex Forbes.
Front L-R: May Miller, Brenda Horne, George Sutherland, Col. Palmer, George Andrew, Nancy McFadden, Mrs Alice Andrew, Eba Sell. *(Submitted by Edward Sutherland, Halkirk).*

Partygoer's at the New Year Ball, held in the Rifle Hall, Wick, circa 1960s.
(Submitted by Maurice Harrington).

Income Tax supper dance, Wick, held in the mid fifties.
(Submitted by Maurice Harrington).

Former pupils' ball, Wick High School, circa 1960.
(Submitted by Maurice Harrington).

Christmas night 1962 at the Seaview Hotel, John O'Groats. *(Submitted by Maurice Harrington).*

Dinner dance in the Seaview Hotel, John O'Groats, circa 1960.

From the family album

Jack Gunn, Achalone, by Halkirk, with his brand new Sunbeam car, about to take the family for a spin, circa 1925.
(Submitted by James Gunn jnr., Gerston).

The Gunn family, Achalone, by Halkirk, enjoying a day trip at John O'Groats. Extreme right: Alex Gunn J.P. vice convener of Caithness, circa 1920.
(Submitted by James Gunn jnr., Gerston)

Royal Air Force Pilot, Lieut Jack (John) Gunn, Achalone, by Halkirk, preparing for take-off in his Camel Sopworth Biplane. Jack is father of Iain A. Gunn of Banniskirk, the present Commander of the Clan Gunn.
(Submitted by James Gunn jnr., Gerston)

Enjoying a day trip to John O'Groats, friends of Donald Gunn, Achalone by Halkirk, strike a pose with his wife, Alexandrina (right), circa 1928.
(Submitted by James Gunn jnr., Gerston).

Right: The Swanson family, Philips Mains, Mey, climbing on board a gig pulled by a Highland pony, circa 1920. A ladies shopping trip? *(Submitted by Margaret Gunn, Gerston)*

Left: An unknown rider on his Norton motorbike, (a friend of the Gunns), taken at Achalone Farm, by Halkirk, owned by Alex Gunn, vice-convener of Caithness, circa 1925.
(Submitted by James Gunn jnr, Gerston).

Right: Enjoying a day trip out west, driver and passenger unknown with Isobel Gunn, wife of James B. Gunn, Gerston, with her brother-in-law, William Gunn. *(Submitted by James Gunn jnr, Gerston).*

Two sets of Manson twins
Left to right: Dennis, Derry, Billy, Alan, Donny and Betty Simpson, circa 1942.
(Submitted by D. Manson).

John Manson, Stroma, at the Henderson Home, late 1920s.

At 'Esperanza', Halkirk, 1967. Back L-R: Ken and Margaret Mackenzie, Ava and Willie Wilson, James, myself (Linda), Andrew, William and Elizabeth Munro. *(Submitted by Linda Munro, Halkirk.*

1965 at Dale Farm, James and Andrew Munro. *(Submitted by Linda Munro, Halkirk).*

Left to right: Four of the eight Gunn brothers Bob, Ben, Donald and Pat, of Achalone, Halkirk with two of the farm horses and farm dog. They are the sons of Alexander Gunn, J.P. and vice convener of Caithness and Margaret Gunn. *(Submitted by James Gunn jnr, Gerston).*

Left: Betty Manson, Wick Pipe Band, 1953.
(Submitted by D. Manson).

Below: Betty and Kathleen Manson,
Wick Pipe Band, 1955
(Submitted by D. Manson)

Left: Pat Gunn, Achalone, by Halkirk, lines up for a shot at Thurso golf course. A suit, tie and plus fours being the dress code.
(Submitted by James Gunn jnr, Gerston).

Left: Vida Shearer and Betty Manson head the parade of the Wick Girls Pipe Band in 1954. *(Submitted by D. Manson).*

Wick Girls Pipe Band taken in 1952. *(Submitted by D. Manson).*

Which way?
James Davidson points the way in the 1950s.
(Submitted by Mrs I. Ferrier, Thurso).

Above: Open air meeting at John O'Groats with Rev. Creelman playing the organ, 1930s.
(Submitted by D. Manson).

Left: Sister Betty sitting in her first car, an MG Midget, in 1957.
(Submitted by D. Manson).

Left: Staff at the Henderson Memorial Nursing Home, Wick, late 1920s.
(Submitted by D. Manson).

Middle: Jane and Katherine Manson, 1953.
(Submitted by D. Manson).

Right: Mrs Bannerman, Mrs Gunn, Mrs Bain and Mrs Mackenzie at back.
(Submitted by Mrs I. Ferrier, Thurso).

Left: Visiting Day at the Henderson Memorial Nursing Home, Wick, late 1920s.
(Submitted by D. Manson).

Mr James Sutherland, the well-known and courteous carrier between Castletown and Thurso, retires after being thirty four years on the road.
(Submitted by Tom Gunn, Marlow).

Granny and Grandfather James Munro, Houstry. (Submitted by Linda Munro).

Canisbay school run, 1950s. (Submitted by Catherine Begg, Thurso).

Alexander Cormack on his croft at Huna in 1930s. (Submitted by Catherine Begg, Thurso).

Left: Wedding of William Munro, Houstry and Elizabeth Gunn, with best man, Angus Munro, (brother) and bridesmaid.
(Submitted by L. Munro, Halkirk).

William and Georgina Swanson, Mey, grandparents of Margaret Gunn (née Mackay), Gerston, Halkirk.
(Submitted by Margaret Gunn, Gerston).

Billy Manson testing the Bristol car engine installed in his motor boat, *Lulu*, in Wick harbour, circa 1965.
(Submitted by D. Manson).

A youthful Johnnie Bain pictured at the ice factory, Wick, circa 1960. *(Submitted by J. & V. Sutherland, Lyth).*

Wick Fire Brigade pumping out the dredger *Badger* in 1964. She was sold in that year for £40, beached and broken up at Papigoe.

Picture taken some of the Territorials of Ross Battery Light Ack Ack Regiment stationed at Wick Airport Drill Hall in 1955. Present at that time were, front row: Sgt. Major Sandy Mcleod, Army Sgt. Major Psi Frank Potter, Sgt. Murray Harper, Major James Mackenzie, C.O. Sgt. Hugh Mackay. Second row: Sgt. Billy Banks, Bdr. Jim McDougall, Bdr. Sandy Alexander, Sgt. Micky Miller, Bdr. George Dick Mackay, Lc Bdr. Dvr. Dan Miller, Lc. Bdr. John George Mackay, Bdr. Henry Durrand, Bdr. Drew Farquhar, Bdr. Donald Grant, Bdr. Dan Harper, Bdr. Donald Harper. Bdr name unknown. The late Major Mackenzie who was C.O. was a weel kent face in Wick for many years through his work and many activities. *(Submitted by Dan Miller, Wick).*

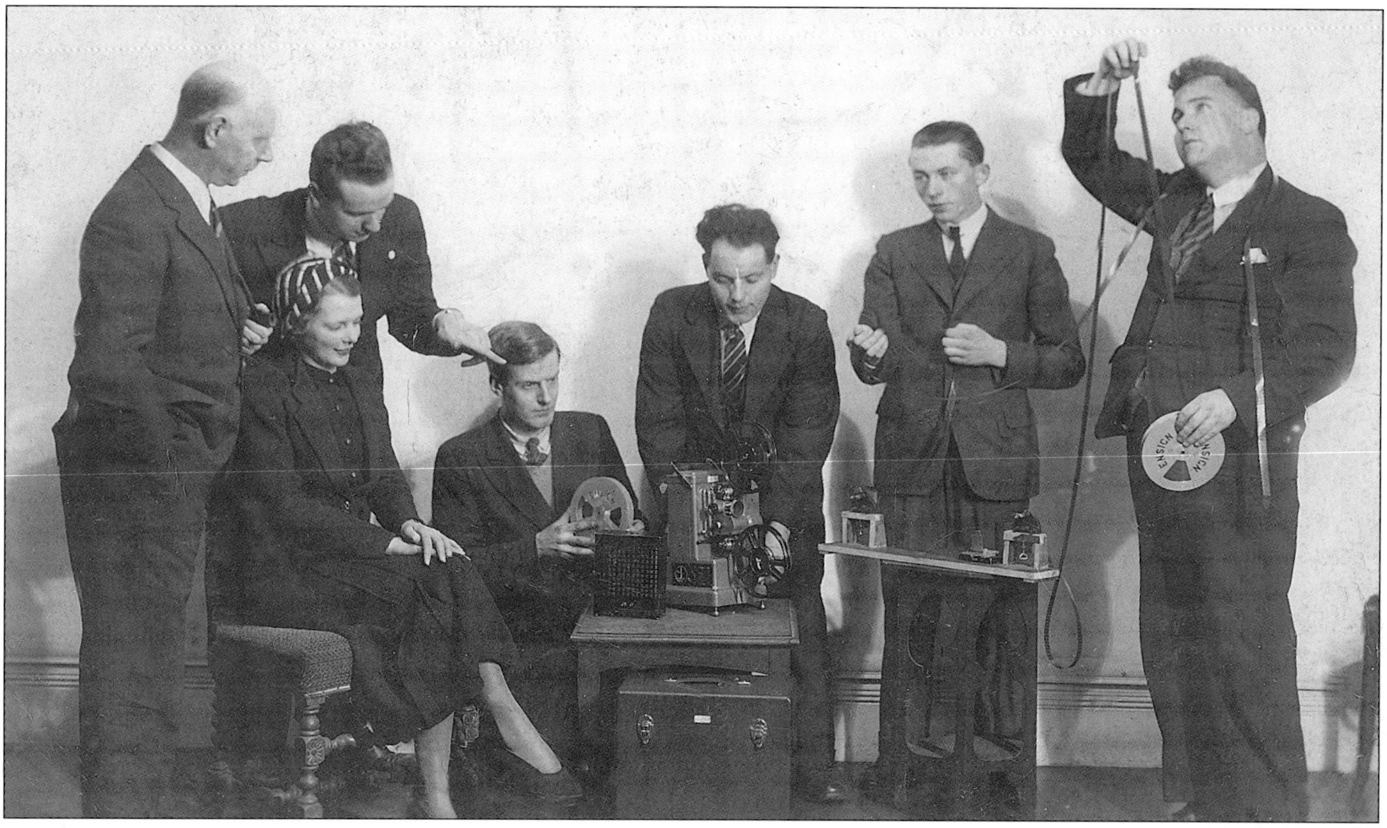

L-R: Col McHardy, next two unknown, Alec Johnston, Johnny Bain, Sinclair Lyle and Jack Faint.
(Submitted by J. & V. Sutherland, Lyth).

Castletown Jazz Band, circa 1940. *(Submitted by Mrs I. Ferrier, Thurso).*

Pictured, circa 1906, behind the Station Hotel, Thurso is James Munro and his wife, Annie, Houstry, Halkirk, with their five children. (Submitted by Tom Munro, Halkirk).

James William Sutherland (pictured right) in front of the Station Hotel, Thurso, was a local carrier between Castletown and Thurso, circa 1920s.*(Submitted by Tom Gunn, Marlow).*

Circa 1952. Sheep clipping at Banniskirk Mains, by Halkirk. George Bremner standing on barrel of beer. 2nd from right, James Gunn, Gerston; 5th from right, James Munro, Houstry; 6th from right, Sandy Munro, Houstry; 7th from right, John Macdonald. It was traditional for neighbouring farmers to help each other out with the clipping. It would last several days and always finished with plenty of drink in celebration. This tradition is dying out as contractors are now brought in. *(Submitted by James Gunn, Halkirk).*

Circa 1954. Caithness Young Farmers float "Altnabreac Peat Fired Power Station". Left to right: Sandy Sinclair, David Pottinger, unknown, unknown, John Calder, James B. Gunn, James Munro, Derry Budge, Master Malcolm. Standing at front: John Campbell, Bunty Calder, Tommy Graham. *(Submitted by John Calder, Thurso).*

Cottages at the top of Princes Street, Thurso, opposite railway station, now demolished (1961/62).
(Submitted by Mrs I. Ferrier, Thurso).

David Alexander pictured at the Riverside, Wick, circa 1928, following his success in the horse and carriage section at the Caithness County Show, Wick. The groom standing right is Mr T. Mulraine and the horse's name was "Peggy".
(Submitted by William Alexander, Thurso).

Wedding of Agnes Heggie (Mey) to George Banks (Mey) at Barrogill Castle. Sitting left to right: Unknown, baby unknown, Jessie Heggie (sister), George Heggie (father), Catherine Westwood Heggie (mother), George Banks (groom), Agnes Heggie (bride), Georgina Heggie (sister and maid of honour), unknown, unknown, unknown, Mary Heggie (sister). 4th from right on back row is William Swanson, who later married Georgina Heggie. Brothers Robert and David Heggie are also in back row. William and Georgina were grandparents of Margaret Gunn (née Mackay), Gerston, Halkirk. The wedding was at the castle as George Heggie was head gardener since 1874. He originated from Anstruther in Fife. The original photo is on display in the Castle of Mey. *(Photo supplied by Margaret Gunn, Gerston, Halkirk)*.

1917. Royal Air Force pilot, James B. Gunn, Achalone, by Halkirk, latterly of Gerston, Halkirk.
(Photo supplied by Margaret Gunn, Gerston).

Staff on the John O'Groat Journal, 1950s. From left to right: Wilma Oag, David Oag (editor) and Georgina Millar, office manager.

The *Groat* girls, wedding guests, 1959. Pictured from left to right: Marie Campbell, Isobel Malcolm, Judy Buchanan, Mina Harper, Sheena Coghill, Georgina Millar and Sheila Coghill.
(Submitted by Maurice Harrington).

The London Caithness Association social gathering at the Royal Scottish Cooperation Hall, Fetter Lane, London, held on Saturday, 30th March, 1940. Pictured standing (top left) Sir Archibald Sinclair accompanied by his lady-in-waiting. *(Photographer: Rawood Ltd, submitted by Stuart Sinclair, Thurso).*

Lipton's Bridge Street store in Wick, circa 1930s with a magnificent display promoting herring fishing in the town. The sign at the front reads, "We have taken STEPS in helping to advertise 'WICK'S STAPLE INDUSTRY'.

A gathering of the Esso Fuel Retailers Association in the late 1950s. Pictured first left standing is Hector Kennedy; third left, Donald Finlayson; fourth left, Teddy Davidson; back row (on left of Esso sign) Bert Dunnet; seventh from right standing, Peter Oman; fifth from right, John King Mowat; second from right, William Bremner. Seated on sofa from left; William Mowatt Snr; Donald Mowatt and Alex Dyer.

This postcard view captured the opening ceremony of the Ross Institute Halkirk in March 1912.

A picture postcard view of Bridge Street, Halkirk, circa 1930.

A happy day at Stemster School picnic. Head teacher is Mr Mackay. Picture taken in the early 1920s.
(Submitted by Hector Polson, Thurso).